K. Langloh Parker

AUSTRALIAN LEGENDS AND MYTHS

UUID: 015db8be-7c3b-11e8-a6cb-17532927e555

This ebook was created with StreetLib Write
 http://write.streetlib.com

Table of contents

PREFACE

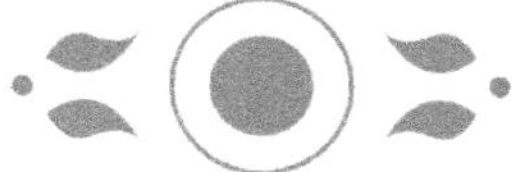

A neighbour of mine exclaimed, when I mentioned that I proposed making a small collection of the folklore legends of the tribe of blacks I knew so well living on this station, "But have the blacks any legends?"—thus showing that people may live in a country, and yet know little of the aboriginal inhabitants; and though there are probably many who do know these particular legends, yet I think that this is the first attempt that has been made to collect the tales of any particular tribe, and publish them alone. At all events, I know that no attempt has been made previously, as far as the folklore of the Noongahburrahs is concerned. Therefore, on the authority of Professor Max Müller, that folk-lore of any country is worth collecting, I am emboldened to offer my small attempt, at a collection, to the public. There are probably many who, knowing these legends, would not think them worth recording; but, on the other hand, I hope there are many who think, as I do, that we should try, while there is yet time, to gather all the information possible of a race fast dying out, and the origin of which is so obscure. I cannot affect to think that these little legends will do much to remove that obscurity, but undoubtedly a scientific and patient study of the folk-lore throughout Australia would greatly assist thereto. I, alas, am but an amateur, moved to my work by interest in the subject, and in the blacks, of whom I have had some experience.

The time is coming when it will be impossible to make even such a collection as this, for the old blacks are quickly dying out, and the young ones will probably think it beneath the dignity of their so-called civilisation even to remember such old-women's stories. Those who have themselves attempted the study of an unknown folk-lore will be able to appreciate the difficulties a student has to surmount before he can even induce those to talk who have the knowledge he desires. In this, as in so much else, those who are ready to be garrulous know little.

I have confined this little book to the legends of the Narran tribe, known among themselves as Noongahburrahs. It is astonishing to find, within comparatively short distances, a diversity of language and custom. You may even find the same word in different tribes bearing a totally different meaning. Many words, too, have been introduced which the blacks think are English, and the English think are native. Such, for example, as piccaninny, and, as far as these outside blacks are concerned, boomerang is regarded as English, their local word being burren; yet nine out of ten people whom you meet think both are local native words.

Though I have written my little book in the interests of folk-lore, I hope it will gain the attention of, and have some interest for, children—of Australian children, because they will find stories of old friends among the Bush birds; and of English children, because I hope that they will be glad to make new friends, and so establish a free trade between the Australian and English nurseries—wingless, and laughing birds, in exchange for fairy godmothers, and princes in disguise.

I must also acknowledge my great indebtedness to the blacks, who, when once they understood what I wanted to know, were most ready to repeat to me the legends—repeating with the utmost patience, time after time, not only the legends, but the names, that I might manage to spell them so as to be understood when repeated. In particular I should like to mention my indebtedness to Peter Hippi, king of the Noongahburrahs; and to Hippitha, Matah, Barahgurrie, and Beemunny.

I have dedicated my booklet to Peter Hippi, in grateful recognition of his long and faithful service to myself and my husband, which has extended, with few intervals, over a period of twenty years. He, too, is probably the last king of the Noongahburrahs, who are fast dying out, and soon their weapons, bartered by them for tobacco or whisky, alone will prove that they ever existed. It seemed to me a pity that some attempt should not be made to collect the folk-lore of the quickly disappearing tribe—a folk-lore embodying, probably, the thoughts, fancies, and beliefs of the genuine aboriginal race, and which, as such, deserves to be, indeed, as Max Müller says, "might be and ought to be, collected in every part of the world."

The legends were told to me by the blacks themselves, some of whom remember the coming of Mitchellän, as they call Major Mitchell, the explorer of these back creeks. The old blacks laugh now when they tell you how frightened their mothers were of the first wheel tracks they saw. They would not let the children tread on them, but carefully lifted them over, lest their feet should break out in sores, as they were supposed to do if they trod on a snake's track. But with all their fear, little did they realise that the coming of Mitchellän was the beginning of their end, or that fifty years afterwards, from the remnant of their once numerous tribe, would be collected the legends they told in those days to their piccaninnies round their camp-fires, and those legends used to make a Christmas booklet for the children of their white supplanters.

I can only hope that the white children will be as ready to listen to these stories as were, and indeed are, the little piccaninnies, and thus the sale of this booklet be such as to enable me to add frocks and tobacco when I give their Christmas dinner, as is my yearly custom, to the remnant of the Noongahburrahs.

K. LANGLOH PARKER.

INTRODUCTION

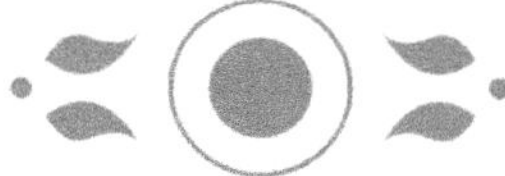

Australia makes an appeal to the fancy which is all its own. When Cortes entered Mexico, in the most romantic moment of history, it was as if men had found their way to a new planet, so strange, so long hidden from Europe was all that they beheld. Still they found kings, nobles, peasants, palaces, temples, a great organised society, fauna and flora not so very different from what they had left behind in Spain. In Australia all was novel, and, while seeming fresh, was inestimably old. The vegetation differs from ours; the monotonous grey gum-trees did not resemble our varied forests, but were antique, melancholy, featureless, like their own continent of rare hills, infrequent streams and interminable deserts, concealing nothing within their wastes, yet promising a secret. The birds and beasts—kangaroo, platypus, emu—are ancient types, rough grotesques of Nature, sketching as a child draws. The natives were a race without a history, far more antique than Egypt, nearer the beginnings than any other people. Their weapons are the most primitive: those of the extinct Tasmanians were actually palæolithic. The soil holds no pottery, the cave walls no pictures drawn by men more advanced; the sea hides no ruined palaces; no cities are buried in the plains; there is not a trace of inscriptions or of agriculture. The burying-places contain relics of men perhaps even lower than the existing tribes; nothing attests the presence in any age of men more cultivated. Perhaps myriads of years have gone by since the Delta, or the lands beside Euphrates and Tigris were as blank of human modification as was the whole Australian continent.

The manners and rites of the natives were far the most archaic of all with which we are acquainted. Temples they had none: no images of gods, no altars of sacrifice; scarce any memorials of the dead. Their worship at best was offered in hymns to some vague, half-forgotten deity or First Maker of things, a god decrepit from age or all but careless of his children. Spirits were known and feared, but scarcely defined or described. Sympathetic magic, and perhaps a little hypnotism, were all their science. Kings and nations they knew not; they were wanderers, houseless and homeless. Custom was king; yet custom was tenacious, irresistible, and as complex in minute details as the etiquette of Spanish kings, or the ritual of the Flamens of Rome. The archaic intricacies and taboos of the customs and regulations of marriage might puzzle a mathematician, and may, when unravelled, explain the less complicated prohibitions of a totemism less antique. The people themselves in their struggle for existence had developed great ingenuities. They had the boomerang and the weet-weet, but not the bow; the throwing stick, but not, of course, the sword; the message stick, but no hieroglyphs; and their art was almost purely decorative, in geometrical patterns, not representative. They deemed themselves akin to all nature, and called cousins with rain and smoke, with clouds and sky, as well as with beasts and trees. They were adroit hunters, skilled trackers, born sportsmen; they now ride well, and, for savages, play cricket fairly. But, being invaded by the practical emigrant or the careless convict, the natives were not studied when in their prime, and science began to examine them almost too late. We have the works of Sir George Grey, the too brief pamphlet of Mr. Gideon Lang, the more learned labours of Messrs. Fison and Howitt, and the collections of Mr. Brough Smyth. The mysteries (Bora) of the natives, the initiatory rites, a little of the magic, a great deal of the social customs are known to us, and we have fragments of the myths. But, till Mrs. Langloh Parker wrote this book, we had but few of the stories which Australian natives tell by the camp-fire or in the gum-tree shade.

These, for the most part, are Kinder Märchen, though they include many ætiological myths, explanatory of the markings and habits of animals, the origin of constellations, and so forth. They are a savage edition of the Metamorphoses, and few unbiased students now doubt that the Metamorphoses are a very late and very artificial version of traditional tales as savage in origin as those of the Noongaburrah. I have read Mrs. Parker's collection with very great interest, with "human pleasure," merely for the story's sake. Children will find here the Jungle Book, never before printed, of black little boys and girls. The sympathy with, and knowledge of beast-life and bird-life are worthy of Mr. Kipling, and the grotesque names are just what children like. Dinewan and Goomblegubbon should take their place with Rikki Tikki and Mr. Kipling's other delightful creatures. But there is here no Mowgli, set apart in the jungle as a man. Man, bird, and beast are all blended in the Australian fancy as in that of Bushmen and Red Indians. All are of one kindred, all shade into each other; all obey the Bush Law as they obey the Jungle Law in Mr. Kipling's fascinating stories. This confusion, of course, is not peculiar to Australian Märchen. it is the prevalent feature of our own popular tales. But the Australians "do it more natural:" the stories are not the heritage of a traditional and dead, but the flowers of a living and actual condition of the mind. The stories have not the ingenious dramatic turns of our own Märchen. Where there are no distinctions of wealth and rank, there can be no Cinderella and no Puss in Boots. Many stories are rude ætiological myths; they explain the habits and characteristics of the birds and beasts, and account in a familiar way for the origin of death ("Bahloo, the Moon, and the Daens"). The origin of fire is also accounted for in what may almost be called a scientific way. Once discovered it is, of course, stolen from the original proprietors. A savage cannot believe that the first owners of fire would give the secret away. The inventors of the myth of Prometheus were of the same mind.

On the whole the stories, perhaps, most resemble those from the

Zulu in character, though these represent a much higher grade of civilisation. The struggle for food and water, desperately absorbing, is the perpetual theme, and no wonder, for the narrators dwell in a dry and thirsty land, and till not, nor sow, nor keep any domestic animals. We see the cunning of the savage in the devices for hunting, especially for chasing honey bees. The Rain-magic, actually practised, is of curious interest. In brief, we have pictures of savage life by savages, romances which are truly realistic. We understand that condition which Dr. Johnson did not think happy—the state from which we came, and to which we shall probably return. "Equality," "Liberty," "Community of Goods," all mean savagery, and even savages, if equal, are not really free. Custom is the tyrant.

The designs are from the sketch-book of an untaught Australian native; they were given to me some years ago by my brother, Dr. Lang, of Corowa. The artist has a good deal of spirit in his hunting scenes; his trees are not ill done, his emus and kangaroos are better than his men and labras. Using ink, a pointed stick, and paper, the artist shows an unwonted freedom of execution. Nothing like this occurs in Australian scratches with a sharp stone on hard wood. Probably no other member of his dying race ever illustrated a book.

ANDREW LANG.

DINEWAN THE EMU, AND GOOMBLEGUBBON THE BUSTARD

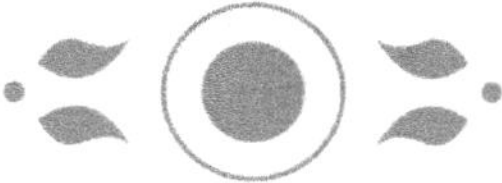

Dinewan the emu, being the largest bird, was acknowledged as king by the other birds. The Goomblegubbons, the bustards, were jealous of the Dinewans. Particularly was Goomblegubbon, the mother, jealous of the Dinewan mother. She would watch with envy the high flight of the Dinewans, and their swift running. And she always fancied that the Dinewan mother flaunted her superiority in her face, for whenever Dinewan alighted near Goomblegubbon, after a long, high flight, she would flap her big wings and begin booing in her pride, not the loud booing of the male bird, but a little, triumphant, satisfied booing noise of her own, which never failed to irritate Goomblegubbon when she heard it.

Goomblegubbon used to wonder how she could put an end to Dinewan's supremacy. She decided that she would only be able to do so by injuring her wings and checking her power of flight. But the question that troubled her was how to effect this end. She knew she would gain nothing by having a quarrel with Dinewan and fighting her, for no Goomblegubbon would stand any chance against a Dinewan. There was evidently nothing to be gained by an open fight. She would have to effect her end by cunning.

One day, when Goomblegubbon saw in the distance Dinewan coming towards her, she squatted down and doubled in her wings in such a way as to look as if she had none. After Dinewan had been talking to her for some time, Goomblegubbon said: "Why do you not imitate me and do without wings? Every bird flies. The Dinewans, to be the king of birds, should do without wings. When all the birds see that I can do without wings, they will think I am the cleverest bird and they will make a Goomblegubbon king."

"But you have wings," said Dinewan.

"No, I have no wings." And indeed she looked as if her words were true, so well were her wings hidden, as she squatted in the grass. Dinewan went away after awhile, and thought much of what she had heard. She talked it all over with her mate, who was as disturbed as she was. They made up their minds that it would never do to let the Goomblegubbons reign in their stead, even if they had to lose their wings to save their kingship.

At length they decided on the sacrifice of their wings. Dinewan mother showed the example by persuading her mate to cut off hers with a combo or stone tomahawk, and then she did the same to his. As soon as the operations were over, the Dinewan mother lost no time in letting Goomblegubbon know what they had done. She ran swiftly down to the plain on which she had left Goomblegubbon, and, finding her still squatting there, she said: "See, I have followed your example. I have now no wings. They are cut off."

"Ha! ha! ha!" laughed Goomblegubbon, jumping up and dancing round with joy at the success of her plot. As she danced round, she spread out her wings, flapped them, and said: "I have taken you in, old stumpy wings. I have my wings yet. You are fine birds, you Dinewans, to be chosen kings, when you are so easily taken in. Ha! ha! ha!" And, laughing derisively, Goomblegubbon flapped her wings right in front of Dinewan, who rushed towards her to chastise her treachery. But Goomblegubbon flew away, and, alas, the now wingless Dinewan could not follow her.

Brooding over her wrongs, Dinewan walked away, vowing she would be revenged. But how? That was the question which she and her mate failed to answer for some time. At length Dinewan mother thought of a plan and prepared at once to execute it. She hid all her young Dinewans but two, under a big salt bush. Then she walked off to Goomblegubbons' plain with the two young ones following her. As she walked off the Morilla ridge, where her home was, on to the plain, she saw Goomblegubbon out feeding with her twelve young ones.

After exchanging a few remarks in a friendly manner with Goomblegubbon, she said to her, "Why do you not imitate me and only have two children? Twelve are too many to feed. If you keep so many they will never grow big birds like the Dinewans. The food that would make big birds of two would only starve twelve." Goomblegubbon said nothing, but she thought it might be so. It was impossible to deny that the young Dinewans were much bigger than the young Goomblegubbons, and, discontentedly, Goomblegubbon walked away, wondering whether the smallness of her young ones was owing to the number of them being so much greater than that of the Dinewans. It would be grand, she thought, to grow as big as the Dinewans. But she remembered the trick she had played on Dinewan, and she thought that perhaps she was being fooled in her turn. She looked back to where the Dinewans fed, and as she saw how much bigger the two young ones were than any of hers, once more mad envy of Dinewan possessed her. She determined she would not be outdone. Rather would she kill all her young ones but two. She said, "The Dinewans shall not be the king birds of the plains. The Goomblegubbons shall replace them. They shall grow as big as the Dinewans, and shall keep their wings and fly, which now the Dinewans cannot do." And straightway Goomblegubbon killed all her young ones but two. Then back she came to where the Dinewans were still feeding. When Dinewan saw her coming and noticed she had only two young ones with her, she called out: "Where are all your young ones?"

Goomblegubbon answered, "I have killed them, and have only two left. Those will have plenty to eat now, and will soon grow as big as your young ones."

"You cruel mother to kill your children. You greedy mother. Why, I have twelve children and I find food for them all. I would not kill one for anything, not even if by so doing I could get back my wings. There is plenty for all. Look at the emu bush how it covers itself with berries to feed my big family. See how the grasshoppers come hopping round, so that we can catch them and fatten on them."

"But you have only two children."

"I have twelve. I will go and bring them to show you." Dinewan ran off to her salt bush where she had hidden her ten young ones. Soon she was to be seen coming back. Running with her neck stretched forward, her head thrown back with pride, and the feathers of her boobootella swinging as she ran, booming out the while her queer throat noise, the Dinewan song of joy, the pretty, soft-looking little ones with their zebra striped skins, running beside her whistling their baby Dinewan note. When Dinewan reached the place where Goomblegubbon was, she stopped her booing and said in a solemn tone, "Now you see my words are true, I have twelve young ones, as I said. You can gaze at my loved ones and think of your poor murdered children. And while you do so I will tell you the fate of your descendants for ever. By trickery and deceit you lost the Dinewans their wings, and now for evermore, as long as a Dinewan has no wings, so long shall a Goomblegubbon lay only two eggs and have only two young ones. We are quits now. You have your wings and I my children."

And ever since that time a Dinewan, or emu, has had no wings, and

a Goomblegubbon, or bustard of the plains, has laid only two eggs in
a season.

THE GALAH, AND OOLAH THE LIZARD

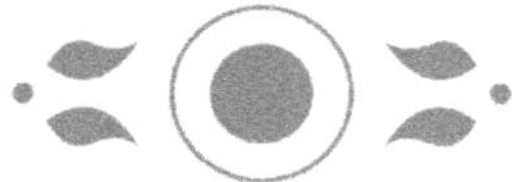

Oolah the lizard was tired of lying in the sun, doing nothing. So he said, "I will go and play." He took his boomerangs out, and began to practise throwing them. While he was doing so a Galah came up, and stood near, watching the boomerangs come flying back, for the kind of boomerangs Oolah was throwing were the bubberahs. They are smaller than others, and more curved, and when they are properly thrown they return to the thrower, which other boomerangs do not.

Oolah was proud of having the gay Galah to watch his skill. In his pride he gave the bubberah an extra twist, and threw it with all his might. Whizz, whizzing through the air back it came, hitting, as it passed her, the Galah on the top of her head, taking both feathers and skin clean off. The Galah set up a hideous, cawing, croaking shriek, and flew about, stopping every few minutes to knock her head on the ground like a mad bird. Oolah was so frightened when he saw what he had done, and noticed that the blood was flowing from the Galah's head, that he glided away to hide under a bindeah bush. But the Galah saw him. She never stopped the hideous noise she was making for a minute, but, still shrieking, followed Oolah. When she reached the bindeah bush she rushed at Oolah, seized him with her beak, rolled him on the bush until every bindeah had made a hole in his skin. Then she rubbed his skin with her own bleeding head. "Now then," she said, "you Oolah shall carry bindeahs on you always, and the stain of my blood."

"And you," said Oolah, as he hissed with pain from the tingling of the prickles, "shall be a bald-headed bird as long as I am a red prickly lizard."

So to this day, underneath the Galah's crest you can always find the bald patch which the bubberah of Oolah first made. And in the country of the Galahs are lizards coloured reddish brown, and covered with spikes like bindeah prickles.

BAHLOO THE MOON, AND THE DAENS

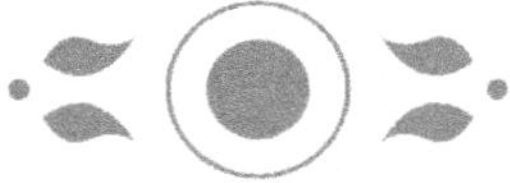

Bahloo the moon looked down at the earth one night, when his light was shining quite brightly, to see if any one was moving. When the earth people were all asleep was the time he chose for playing with his three dogs. He called them dogs, but the earth people called them snakes, the death adder, the black snake, and the tiger snake. As he looked down on to the earth, with his three dogs beside him, Bahloo saw about a dozen daens, or black fellows, crossing a creek. He called to them saying, "Stop, I want you to carry my dogs across that creek." But the black fellows, though they liked Bahloo well, did not like his dogs, for sometimes when he had brought these dogs to play on the earth, they had bitten not only the earth dogs but their masters; and the poison left by the bites had killed those bitten. So the black fellows said, "No, Bahloo, we are too frightened; your dogs might bite us. They are not like our dogs, whose bite would not kill us."

Bahloo said, "If you do what I ask you, when you die you shall come to life again, not die and stay always where you are put when you are dead. See this piece of bark. I throw it into the water." And he threw a piece of bark into the creek. "See it comes to the top again and floats. That is what would happen to you if you would do what I ask you: first under when you die, then up again at once. If you will not take my dogs over, you foolish daens, you will die like this," and he threw a stone into the creek, which sank to the bottom. "You will be like that stone, never rise again, Wombah daens!"

But the black fellows said, "We cannot do it, Bahloo. We are too frightened of your dogs."

"I will come down and carry them over myself to show you that they are quite safe and harmless." And down he came, the black snake coiled round one arm, the tiger snake round the other, and the death adder on his shoulder, coiled towards his neck. He carried them over. When he had crossed the creek he picked up a big stone, and he threw it into the water, saying, "Now, you cowardly daens, you would not do what I, Bahloo, asked you to do, and so forever you have lost the chance of rising again after you die. You will just stay where you are put, like that stone does under the water, and grow, as it does, to be part of the earth. If you had done what I asked you, you could have died as often as I die, and have come to life as often as I come to life. But now you will only be black fellows while you live, and bones when you are dead."

Bahloo looked so cross, and the three snakes hissed so fiercely, that the black fellows were very glad to see them disappear from their sight behind the trees. The black fellows had always been frightened of Bahloo's dogs, and now they hated them, and they said, "If we could get them away from Bahloo we would kill them." And thenceforth, whenever they saw a snake alone they killed it. But Bahloo only sent more, for he said, "As long as there are black fellows there shall be snakes to remind them that they would not do what I asked them."

THE ORIGIN OF THE NARRAN LAKE

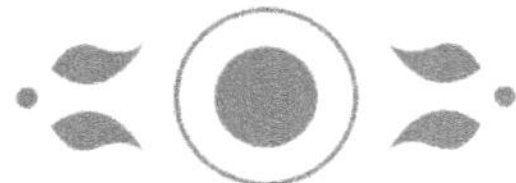

Old Byamee said to his two young wives, Birrahgnooloo and Cunnunbeillee, "I have stuck a white feather between the hind legs of a bee, and am going to let it go and then follow it to its nest, that I may get honey. While I go for the honey, go you two out and get frogs and yams, then meet me at Coorigel Spring, where we will camp, for sweet and clear is the water there." The wives, taking their goolays and yam sticks, went out as he told them. Having gone far, and dug out many yams and frogs, they were tired when they reached Coorigel, and, seeing the cool, fresh water, they longed to bathe. But first they built a bough shade, and there left their goolays holding their food, and the yams and frogs they had found. When their camp was ready for the coming of Byamee, who having wooed his wives with a nullah-nullah, kept them obedient by fear of the same weapon, then went the girls to the spring to bathe. Gladly they plunged in, having first divested themselves of their goomillahs, which they were still young enough to wear, and which they left on the ground near the spring. Scarcely were they enjoying the cool rest the water gave their hot, tired limbs, when they were seized and swallowed by two kurreahs. Having swallowed the girls, the kurreahs dived into an opening in the side of the spring, which was the entrance to an underground watercourse leading to the Narran River. Through this passage they went, taking all the water from the spring with them into the Narran, whose course they also dried as they went along.

Meantime Byamee, unwitting the fate of his wives, was honey hunting. He had followed the bee with the white feather on it for some distance; then the bee flew on to some budtha flowers, and would move no further. Byamee said, "Something has happened, or the bee would not stay here and refuse to be moved on towards its nest. I must go to Coorigel Spring and see if my wives are safe. Something terrible has surely happened." And Byamee turned in haste towards the spring. When he reached there he saw the bough shed his wives had made, he saw the yams they had dug from the ground, and he saw the frogs, but Birrahgnooloo and Cunnunbeillee he saw not. He called aloud for them. But no answer. He went towards the spring; on the edge of it he saw the goomillahs of his wives. He looked into the spring and, seeing it dry, he said, "It is the work of the kurreahs; they have opened the underground passage and gone with my wives to the river, and opening the passage has dried the spring. Well do I know where the passage joins the Narran, and there will I swiftly go." Arming himself with spears and woggarahs he started in pursuit. He soon reached the deep hole where the underground channel of the Coorigel joined the Narran. There he saw what he had never seen before, namely this deep hole dry. And he said: "They have emptied the holes as they went along, taking the water with them. But well know I the deep holes of the river. I will not follow the bend, thus trebling the distance I have to go, but I will cut across from big hole to big hole, and by so doing I may yet get ahead of the kurreahs." On swiftly sped Byamee, making short cuts from big hole to big hole, and his track is still marked by the morilla ridges that stretch down the Narran, pointing in towards the deep holes. Every hole as he came to it he found dry, until at last he reached the end of the Narran; the hole there was still quite wet and muddy, then he knew he was near his enemies, and soon he saw them. He managed to get, unseen, a little way ahead of the kurreahs. He hid himself behind a big dheal tree. As the kurreahs came near they separated, one turning to go in another direction. Quickly Byamee hurled one spear after another, wounding both kurreahs, who writhed with pain and lashed their tails furiously, making great hollows in the ground, which the water they had brought with them quickly filled. Thinking they might again escape him, Byamee drove them from the water with his spears, and then, at close quarters, he killed them with his woggarahs. And ever afterwards at flood time, the Narran flowed into this hollow which the kurreahs in their writhings had made.

When Byamee saw that the kurreahs were quite dead, he cut them open and took out the bodies of his wives. They were covered with wet slime, and seemed quite lifeless; but he carried them and laid them on two nests of red ants. Then he sat down at some little distance and watched them. The ants quickly covered the bodies, cleaned them rapidly of the wet slime, and soon Byamee noticed the muscles of the girls twitching. "Ah," he said, "there is life, they feel the sting of the ants."

Almost as he spoke came a sound as of a thunder-clap, but the sound seemed to come from the ears of the girls. And as the echo was dying away, slowly the girls rose to their feet. For a moment they stood apart, a dazed expression on their faces. Then they clung together, shaking as if stricken with a deadly fear. But Byamee came to them and explained how they had been rescued from the kurreahs by him. He bade them to beware of ever bathing in the deep holes of the Narran, lest such holes be the haunt of kurreahs.

Then he bade them look at the water now at Boogira, and he said:

"Soon will the black swans find their way here, the pelicans and the ducks; where there was dry land and stones in the past, in the future there will be water and water-fowl, from henceforth; when the Narran runs it will run into this hole, and by the spreading of its waters will a big lake be made." And what Byamee said has come to pass, as the Narran Lake shows, with its large sheet of water, spreading for miles, the home of thousands of wild fowl.

GOOLOO THE MAGPIE, AND THE WAHROOGAH

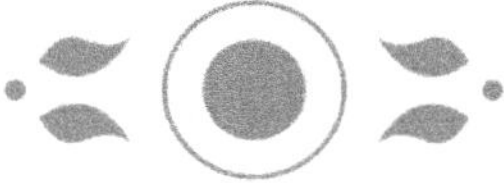

Gooloo was a very old woman, and a very wicked old woman too, as this story will tell. During all the past season, when the grass was thick with seed, she had gathered much doonburr, which she crushed into meal as she wanted it for food. She used to crush it on a big flat stone with small flat stones—the big stone was called a dayoorl. Gooloo ground a great deal of the doonburr seed to put away for immediate use, the rest she kept whole, to be ground as required.

Soon after she had finished her first grinding, a neighbouring tribe came along and camped near where she was. One day the men all went out hunting, leaving the women and the children in the camp. After the men had been gone a little while, Gooloo the magpie came to their camp to talk to the women. She said, "Why do you not go hunting too? Many are the nests of the wurranunnahs round here, and thick is the honey in them. Many and ripe are the bumbles hanging now on the bumble trees; red is the fruit of the grooees, and opening with ripeness the fruit of the guiebets. Yet you sit in the camp and hunger, until your husbands return with the dinewan and bowrah they have gone forth to slay. Go, women, and gather of the plenty that surrounds you. I will take care of your children, the little Wahroogahs."

"Your words are wise," the women said. "It is foolish to sit here and hunger, when near at hand yams are thick in the ground, and many fruits wait but the plucking. We will go and fill quickly our comebees and goolays, but our children we will take with us."

"Not so," said Gooloo, "foolish indeed were you to do that. You would tire the little feet of those that run, and tire yourselves with the burden of those that have to be carried. No, take forth your comebees and goolays empty that ye may bring back the more. Many are the spoils that wait only the hand of the gatherer. Look ye, I have a durrie made of fresh doonburr seed, cooking just now on that bark between two fires; that shall your children eat, and swiftly shall I make them another. They shall eat and be full ere their mothers are out of sight. See, they come to me now, they hunger for durrie, and well will I feed them. Haste ye then, that ye may return in time to make ready the fires for cooking the meat your husbands will bring. Glad will your husbands be when they see that ye have filled your goolays and comebees with fruits, and your wirrees with honey. Haste ye, I say, and do well."

Having listened to the words of Gooloo, the women decided to do as she said, and, leaving their children with her, they started forth with empty comebees, and armed with combos, with which to chop out the bees' nests and opossums, and with yam sticks to dig up yams.

When the women had gone, Gooloo gathered the children round her and fed them with durrie, hot from the coals. Honey too, she gave them, and bumbles which she had buried to ripen. When they had eaten, she hurried them off to her real home, built in a hollow tree, a little distance away from where she had been cooking her durrie. Into her house she hurriedly thrust them, followed quickly herself, and made all secure. Here she fed them again, but the children had already satisfied their hunger, and now they missed their mothers and began to cry. Their crying reached the ears of the women as they were returning to their camp. Quickly they came at the sound which is not good in a mother's ears. As they quickened their steps they thought how soon the spoils that lay heavy in their comebees would comfort their children. And happy they, the mothers, would feel when they fed the Wahroogahs with the dainties they had gathered for them. Soon they reached the camp, but, alas! where were their children? And where was Gooloo the magpie?

"They are playing wahgoo," they said, "and have hidden themselves."

The mothers hunted all round for them, and called aloud the names of their children and Gooloo. But no answer could they hear and no trace could they find. And yet every now and then they heard the sound of children wailing. But seek as they would they found them not. Then loudly wailed the mothers themselves for their lost Wahroogahs, and, wailing, returned to the camp to wait the coming of the black fellows. Heavy were their hearts, and sad were their faces when their husbands returned. They hastened to tell the black fellows when they came, how Gooloo had persuaded them to go hunting, promising if they did so that she would feed the hungry Wahroogahs, and care for them while they were away, but—and here they wailed again for their poor Wahroogahs. They told how they had listened to her words and gone; truth had she told of the plenty round, their comebees and goolays were full of fruits and spoils they had gathered, but, alas, they came home with them laden only to find their children gone and Gooloo gone too. And no trace could they find of either, though at times they heard a sound as of children wailing.

Then wroth were the men, saying: "What mothers are ye to leave your young to a stranger, and that stranger a Gooloo, ever a treacherous race? Did we not go forth to gain food for you and our children? Saw ye ever your husbands return from the chase empty handed? Then why, when ye knew we were gone hunting, must ye too go forth and leave our helpless ones to a stranger? Oh, evil, evil indeed is the time that has come when a mother forgets her child. Stay ye in the camp while we go forth to hunt for our lost Wahroogahs. Heavy will be our hands on the women if we return without them."

The men hunted the bush round for miles, but found no trace of the lost Wahroogahs, though they too heard at times a noise as of children's voices wailing.

But beyond the wailing which echoed in the mothers' ears for ever, no trace was found of the children. For many days the women sat in the camp mourning for their lost Wahroogahs, and beating their heads because they had listened to the voice of Gooloo.

THE WEEOOMBEENS AND THE PIGGIEBILLAH

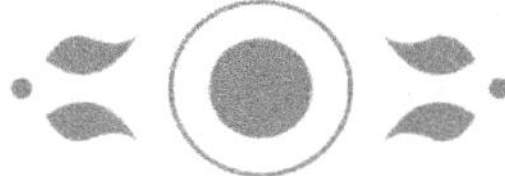

Two Weeoombeen brothers went out hunting. One brother was much younger than the other and smaller, so when they sighted an emu, the elder one said to the younger: "You stay quietly here and do not make a noise, or Piggiebillah, whose camp we passed just now, will hear you and steal the emu if I kill it. He is so strong. I'll go on and try to kill the emu with this stone." The little Weeoombeen watched his big brother sneak up to the emu, crawling, along almost flat, on the ground. He saw him get quite close to the emu, then spring up quickly and throw the stone with such an accurate aim as to kill the bird on the spot. The little brother was so rejoiced that he forgot his brother's caution, and he called aloud in his joy. The big Weeoombeen looked round and gave him a warning sign, but too late, Piggiebillah had heard the cry and was hastening towards them. Quickly big Weeoombeen left the emu and joined his little brother.

Piggiebillah when he came up, said: "What have you found?"

"Nothing," said the big Weeoombeen, "nothing but some mistletoe berries."

"It must have been something more than that, or your little brother would not have called out so loudly."

Little Weeoombeen was so afraid that Piggiebillah would find their emu and take it, that he said: "I hit a little bird with a stone, and I was glad I could throw so straight."

"It was no cry for the killing of a little bird or for the finding of mistletoe berries that I heard. It was for something much more than either, or you would not have called out so joyfully. If you do not tell me at once I will kill you both."

The Weeoombeen brothers were frightened, for Piggiebillah was a great fighter and very strong, so when they saw he was really angry, they showed him the dead emu.

"Just what I want for my supper," he said, and so saying, dragged it away to his own camp. The Weeoombeens followed him and even helped him to make a fire to cook the emu, hoping by so doing to get a share given to them. But Piggiebillah would not give them any; he said he must have it all for himself.

Angry and disappointed, the Weeoombeens marched straight off and told some black fellows who lived near, that Piggiebillah had a fine fat emu just cooked for supper.

Up jumped the black fellows, seized their spears, bade the Weeoombeens quickly lead them to Piggiebillah's camp, promising them for so doing, a share of the emu.

When they were within range of spear shot, the black fellows formed a circle, took aim, and threw their spears at Piggiebillah. As the spears fell thick on him, sticking out all over him, Piggiebillah cried aloud: "Bingehlah, Bingehlah. You can have it, you can have it." But the black fellows did not desist until Piggiebillah was too wounded even to cry out; then they left him a mass of spears and turned to look for the emu. But to their surprise they found it not. Then for the first time they missed the Weeoombeens.

Looking round they saw their tracks going to where the emu had evidently been; then they saw that they had dragged the emu to their nyunnoo, which was a humpy made of grass.

When the Weeoombeens saw the black fellows coming, they caught hold of the emu and dragged it to a big hole they knew of, with a big stone at its entrance, which stone only they knew the secret of moving. They moved the stone, got the emu and themselves into the hole, and the stone in place again before the black fellows reached the place.

The black fellows tried to move the stone, but could not. Yet they knew that the Weeoombeens must have done so, for they had tracked them right up to it, and they could hear the sound of their voices on the other side of it. They saw there was a crevice on either side of the stone, between it and the ground. Through these crevices they drove in their spears, thinking they must surely kill the brothers. But the Weeoombeens too had seen these crevices and had anticipated the spears, so they had placed the dead emu before them to act as a shield. And into its body were driven the spears of the black fellows intended for the Weeoombeens.

Having driven the spears well in, the black fellows went off to get help to move the stone, but when they had gone a little way they heard the Weeoombeens laughing. Back they came and speared again, and again started for help, only as they left to hear once more the laughter of the brothers.

The Weeoombeens finding their laughter only brought back the black fellows to a fresh attack, determined to keep quiet, which, after the next spearing, they did.

Quite sure, when they heard their spear shots followed by neither conversation nor laughter, that they had killed the Weeoombeens at last, the black fellows hurried away to bring back the strength and cunning of the camp, to remove the stone.

The Weeoombeens hurriedly discussed what plan they had better adopt to elude the black fellows, for well they knew that should they ever meet any of them again they would be killed without mercy. And as they talked they satisfied their hunger by eating some of the emu flesh.

After a while the black fellows returned, and soon was the stone removed from the entrance. Some of them crept into the hole, where, to their surprise, they found only the remains of the emu and no trace of the Weeoombeens. As those who had gone in first, crept out and told of the disappearance of the Weeoombeens, others, incredulous of such a story, crept in to find it confirmed. They searched round for tracks; seeing that their spears were all in the emu it seemed to them probable the Weeoombeens had escaped alive, but if so, whither they had gone their tracks would show. But search as they would no tracks could they find. All they could see were two little birds which sat on a bush near the hole, watching the black fellows all the time. The little birds flew round the hole sometimes, but never away, always returning to their bush and seeming to be discussing the whole affair; but what they said the black fellows could not understand. But as time went on and no sign was ever found of the Weeoombeens, the black fellows became sure that the brothers had turned into the little white-throated birds which had sat on the bush by the hole, so, they supposed, to escape their vengeance. And ever afterwards the little white-throats were called Weeoombeens. And the memory of Piggiebillah is perpetuated by a sort of porcupine ant eater, which bears his name, and whose skin is covered closely with miniature spears sticking all over it.

BOOTOOLGAH THE CRANE AND GOONUR THE KANGAROO RAT, THE FIRE MAKERS

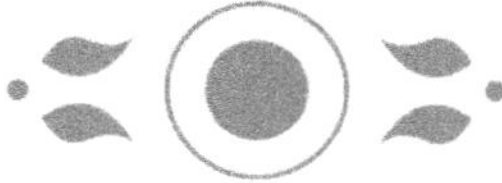

In the days when Bootoolgah, the crane, married Goonur, the kangaroo rat, there was no fire in their country. They had to eat their food raw or just dry it in the sun. One day when Bootoolgah was rubbing two pieces of wood together, he saw a faint spark sent forth and then a slight smoke. "Look," he said to Goonur, "see what comes when I rub these pieces of wood together—smoke! Would it not be good if we could make fire for ourselves with which to cook our food, so as not to have to wait for the sun to dry it?"

Goonur looked, and, seeing the smoke, she said: "Great indeed would be the day when we could make fire. Split your stick, Bootoolgah, and place in the opening bark and grass that even one spark may kindle a light." And hearing wisdom in her words, even as she said Bootoolgah did. And lo! after much rubbing, from the opening came a small flame. For as Goonur had said it would, the spark lit the grass, the bark smouldered and smoked, and so Bootoolgah the crane, and Goonur the kangaroo rat, discovered the art of fire making.

"This we will keep secret," they said, "from all the tribes. When we make a fire to cook our fish we will go into a Bingahwingul scrub. There will we make a fire and cook our food in secret. We will hide our fire sticks in the open-mouthed seeds of the Bingahwinguls; one fire stick we will carry always hidden in our comebee."

Bootoolgah and Goonur cooked the next fish they caught, and found it very good. When they went back to the camp they took some of their cooked fish with them. The blacks noticed it looked quite different from the usual sundried fish, so they asked: "What did you to that fish?"

"Let it lie in the sun," said they.

"Not so," said the others.

But that the fish was sundried Bootoolgah and Goonur persisted. Day by day passed, and after catching their fish, these two always disappeared, returning with their food looking quite different from that of the others. At last, being unable to extract any information from them, it was determined by the tribe to watch them. Boolooral, the night owl, and Quarrian, the parrot, were appointed to follow the two when they disappeared, to watch where they went, and find out what they did. Accordingly, after the next fish were caught, when Bootoolgah and Goonur gathered up their share and started for the bush, Boolooral and Quarrian followed on their tracks. They saw them disappear into a Bingahwingul scrub, where they lost sight of them. Seeing a high tree on the edge of the scrub, they climbed up it, and from there they saw all that was to be seen. They saw Bootoolgah and Goonur throw down their load of fish, open their comebee and take from it a stick, which stick, when they had blown upon it, they laid in the midst of a heap of leaves and twigs, and at once from this heap they saw a flame leap, which flame the fire makers fed with bigger sticks. Then, as the flame died down, they saw the two place- their fish in the ashes that remained from the burnt sticks. Then back to the camp of their tribes went Boolooral and Quarrian, back with the news of their discovery. Great was the talk amongst the blacks, and many the queries as to how to get possession of the comebee with the fire stick in it, when next Bootoolgah and Goonur came into the camp. It was at length decided to hold a corrobboree, and it was to be one on a scale not often seen, probably never before by the young of the tribes. The grey beards proposed to so astonish Bootoolgah and Goonur as to make them forget to guard their precious comebee. As soon as they were intent on the corrobboree and off guard, some one was to seize the comebee, steal the firestick and start fires for the good of all. Most of them had tasted the cooked fish brought into the camp by the fire makers and, having found it good, hungered for it. Beeargah, the hawk, was told to feign sickness, to tie up his head, and to lie down near wherever the two sat to watch the corrobboree. Lying near them, he was to watch them all the time, and when they were laughing and unthinking of anything but the spectacle before them, he was to steal the comebee. Having arranged their plan of action, they all prepared for a big corrobboree. They sent word to all the surrounding tribes, asking them to attend, especially they begged the Bralgahs to come, as they were celebrated for their wonderful dancing, which was so wonderful as to be most likely to absorb the attention of the fire makers.

All the tribes agreed to come, and soon all were engaged in great preparations. Each determined to outdo the other in the quaintness and brightness of their painting for the corrobboree. Each tribe as they arrived gained great applause; never before had the young people seen so much diversity in colouring and design. Beeleer, the black cockatoo tribe, came with bright splashes of orange-red on their black skins. The Pelicans came as a contrast, almost pure white, only a touch here and there of their black skin showing where the white paint had rubbed off. The Black Divers came in their black skins, but these polished to shine like satin. Then came the Millears, the beauties of the Kangaroo Rat family, who had their home on the Morillas. After them came the Buckandeer or Native Cat tribe, painted in dull colours, but in all sorts of patterns. Mairas or Paddymelons came too in haste to take part in the great corrobboree. After them, walking slowly, came the Bralgahs, looking tall and dignified as they held up their red heads, painted so in contrast to their French-grey bodies, which they deemed too dull a colour, unbrightened, for such a gay occasion. Amongst the many tribes there, too numerous to mention, were the rose and grey painted Galahs, the green and crimson painted Billai: most brilliant were they with their bodies grass green and their sides bright crimson, so afterwards gaining them the name of crimson wings. The bright little Gidgereegahs came too.

Great was the gathering that Bootoolgah, the crane, and Goonur, the kangaroo rat, found assembled as they hurried on to the scene. Bootoolgah had warned Goonur that they must only be spectators, and take no active part in the corrobboree, as they had to guard their comebee. Obedient to his advice, Goonur seated herself beside him and slung the comebee over her arm. Bootoolgah warned her to be careful and not forget she had it. But as the corrobboree went on, so absorbed did she become that she forgot the comebee, which slipped from her arm. Happily, Bootoolgah saw it do so, replaced it, and bade her take heed, so baulking Beeargah, who had been about to seize it, for his vigilance was unceasing, and, deeming him sick almost unto death, the two whom he was watching took no heed of him. Back he crouched, moaning as he turned, but keeping ever an eye on Goonur. And soon was he rewarded. Now came the turn of the Bralgahs to dance, and every eye but that of the watchful one was fixed on them as slowly they came into the ring. First they advanced, bowed and retired, then they repeated what they had done before, and again, each time getting faster and faster in their movements, changing their bows into pirouettes, craning their long necks and making such antics as they went through the figures of their dance, and replacing their dignity with such grotesqueness, as to make their large audience shake with laughter, they themselves keeping throughout all their grotesque measures a solemn air, which only seemed to heighten the effect of their antics.

And now came the chance of Beeargah the hawk. In the excitement of the moment Goonur forgot the comebee, as did Bootoolgah. They joined in the mirthful applause of the crowd, and Goonur threw herself back helpless with laughter. As she did so the comebee slipped from her arm. Then up jumped the sick man from behind her, seized the comebee with his combo, cut it open, snatched forth the firestick, set fire to the heap of grass ready near where he had lain, and all before the two realised their loss. When they discovered the precious comebee was gone, up jumped Bootoolgar and Goonur. After Beeargah ran Bootoolgah, but Beeargah had a start and was fleeter of foot, so distanced his pursuer quickly. As he ran he fired the grass with the stick he still held. Bootoolgar, finding he could not catch Beeargah, and seeing fires everywhere, retired from the pursuit, feeling it was useless now to try and guard their secret, for it had now become the common property of all the tribes there assembled.

WEEDAH THE MOCKING BIRD

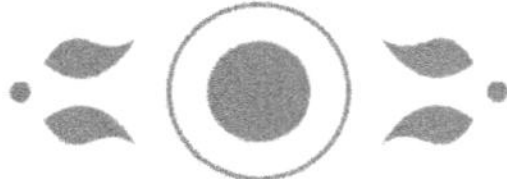

Weedah was playing a great trick on the black fellows who lived near him. He had built himself a number of grass nyunnoos, more than twenty. He made fires before each, to make it look as if some one lived in the nyunnoos. First he would go into one nyunnoo, or humpy, and cry like a baby, then to another and laugh like a child, then in turn as he went the round of the humpies he would sing like a maiden, corrobboree like a man, call out in a quavering voice like an old man, and in a shrill voice like an old woman; in fact, imitate any sort of voice he had ever heard, and imitate them so quickly in succession that any one passing would think there was a great crowd of blacks in that camp. His object was to entice as many strange black fellows into his camp as he could, one at a time; then he would kill them and gradually gain the whole country round for his own. His chance was when he managed to get a single black fellow into his camp, which he very often did, then by his cunning he always gained his end and the black fellow's death. This was how he attained that end. A black fellow, probably separated from his fellows in the excitement of the chase, would be returning home alone; passing within ear shot of Weedah's camp he would hear the various voices and wonder what tribe could be there. Curiosity would induce him to come near. He would probably peer into the camp, and, only seeing Weedah standing alone, would advance towards him. Weedah would be standing at a little distance from a big glowing fire, where he would wait until the strange black fellow came quite close to him. Then he would ask him what he wanted. The stranger would say he had heard many voices and had wondered what tribe it could be, so had come near to find out. Weedah would say, "But only I am here. How could you have heard voices? See; look round, I am alone." Bewildered, the stranger would look round and say in a puzzled tone of voice: "Where are they all gone? As I came I heard babies crying, men calling, and women laughing; many voices I heard but you only I see."

"And only I am here. The wind must have stirred the branches of the balah trees, and you must have thought it was the wailing of children, the laughing of the gouggourgahgah you heard, and thought it the laughter of women, and mine must have been the voice as of men that you heard. Alone in the bush, as the shadows fall, a man breeds strange fancies. See by the light of this fire, where are your fancies now? No women laugh, no babies cry, only I, Weedah, talk." As Weedah was talking he kept edging the stranger towards the fire; when they were quite close to it, he turned swiftly, seized him, and threw him right into the middle of the blaze. This scene was repeated time after time, until at last the ranks of the black fellows living round the camp of Weedah, began to get thin.

Mullyan, the eagle hawk, determined to fathom the mystery, for as yet the black fellows had no clue as to how or where their friends had disappeared. Mullyan, when Beeargah, his cousin, returned to his camp no more, made up his mind to get on his track and follow it, until at length he solved the mystery. After following the track of Beeargah, as he had chased the kangaroo to where he had slain it, on he followed his homeward trail. Over stony ground he tracked him, and through sand, across plains, and through scrub. At last in a scrub and still on the track of Beeargah, he heard the sounds of many voices, babies crying, women singing, men talking. Peering through the bush, finding the track took him nearer the spot whence came the sounds, he saw the grass humpies. "Who can these be?" he thought. The track led him right into the camp, where alone Weedah was to be seen. Mullyan advanced towards him and asked where were the people whose voices he had heard as he came through the bush.

Weedah said: "How can I tell you? I know of no people; I live alone."

"But," said Mullyan the eagle hawk, "I heard babies crying, women laughing, and men talking, not one but many."

"And I alone am here. Ask of your ears what trick they played you, or perhaps your eyes fail you now. Can you see any but me? Look for yourself."

"And if, as indeed it seems, you only are here, what did you with Beeargah my cousin, and where are my friends? Many are their trails that I see coming into this camp, but none going out. And if you alone live here you alone can answer me."

"What know I of you or your friends? Nothing. Ask of the winds that blow. Ask of Bahloo the moon, who looks down on the earth by night. Ask of Yhi the sun, that looks down by day. But ask not Weedah, who dwells alone, and knows naught of your friends." But as Weedah was talking he was carefully edging Mullyan towards the fire.

Mullyan, the eagle hawk, too, was cunning, and not easy to trap. He saw a blazing fire in front of him, he saw the track of his friend behind him, he saw Weedah was edging him towards the fire, and it came to him in a moment the thought that if the fire could speak, well could it tell where were his friends. But the time was not yet come to show that he had fathomed the mystery. So he affected to fall into the trap. But when they reached the fire, before Weedah had time to act his usual part, with a mighty grip Mullyan the eagle hawk seized him, saying, "Even as you served Beeargah the hawk, my cousin, and my friends, so now serve I you," And right into the middle of the blazing fire he threw him. Then he turned homewards in haste, to tell the black fellows that he had solved the fate of their friends, which had so long been a mystery. When he was some distance from the Weedah's camp, he heard the sound of a thunder clap. But it was not thunder it was the bursting of the back of Weedah's head, which had burst with a bang as of a thunder clap. And as it burst, out from his remains had risen a bird, Weedah, the mocking bird; which bird to this day has a hole at the back of his head, just in the same place as Weedah the black fellow's head had burst, and whence the bird came forth.

To this day the Weedah makes grass playgrounds, through which he runs, imitating, as he plays, in quick succession, any voices he has ever heard, from the crying of a child to the laughing of a woman; from the mewing of a cat to the barking of a dog, and hence his name Weedah, the mocking bird.

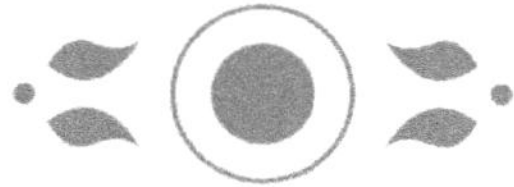

Gwineeboo and Goomai, the water rat, were down at the creek one day, getting mussels for food, when, to their astonishment, a kangaroo hopped right into the water beside them. Well they knew that he must be escaping from hunters, who were probably pressing him close. So Gwineeboo quickly seized her yam stick, and knocked the kangaroo on the head: he was caught fast in the weeds in the creek, so could not escape. When the two old women had killed the kangaroo they hid its body under the weeds in the creek, fearing to take it out and cook it straight away, lest the hunters should come up and claim it. The little son of Gwineeboo watched them from the bank. After having hidden the kangaroo, the women picked up their mussels and started for their camp, when up came the hunters, Quarrian and Gidgereegah, who had tracked the kangaroo right to the creek.

Seeing the women they said: "Did you see a kangaroo?

The women answered: "No. We saw no kangaroo."

"That is strange, for we have tracked it right up to here."

"We have seen no kangaroo. See, we have been digging out mussels for food. Come to our camp, and we will give you some when they are cooked."

The young men, puzzled in their minds, followed the women to their camp, and when the mussels were cooked the hunters joined the old women at their dinner. The little boy would not eat the mussels; he kept crying to his mother, "Gwineeboo, Gwineeboo. I want kangaroo. I want kangaroo. Gwineeboo. Gwineeboo."

"There," said Quarrian. "Your little boy has seen the kangaroo, and wants some; it must be here somewhere."

"Oh, no. He cries for anything he thinks of, some days for kangaroo; he is only a little boy, and does not know what he wants," said old Gwineeboo. But still the child kept saying, "Gwineeboo. Gwineeboo. I want kangaroo. I want kangaroo." Goomai was so angry with little Gwineeboo for keeping on asking for kangaroo, and thereby making the young men suspicious, that she hit him so hard on the mouth to keep him quiet, that the blood came, and trickled down his breast, staining it red. When she saw this, old Gwineeboo grew angry in her turn, and hit old Goomai, who returned the blow, and so a fight began, more words than blows, so the noise was great, the women fighting, little Gwineeboo crying, not quite knowing whether he was crying because Goomai had hit him, because his mother was fighting, or because he still wanted kangaroo.

Quarrian said to Gidgereegah. "They have the kangaroo somewhere hidden; let us slip away now in the confusion. We will only hide, then come back in a little while, and surprise them."

They went quietly away, and as soon as the two women noticed they had gone, they ceased fighting, and determined to cook the kangaroo. They watched the two young men out of sight, and waited some time so as to be sure that they were safe. Then down they hurried to get the kangaroo. They dragged it out, and were just making a big fire on which to cook it, when up came Quarrian and Gidgereegah, saying:

"Ah! we thought so. You had our kangaroo all the time; little Gwineeboo was right."

"But we killed it," said the women.

"But we hunted it here," said the men, and so saying caught hold of
the kangaroo and dragged it away to some distance, where they
made a fire and cooked it. Goomai, Gwineeboo, and her little boy
went over to Quarrian and Gidgereegah, and begged for some of the
meat, but the young men would give them none, though litttle Gwineeboo cried piteously for some. But no; they said they would rather
throw what they did not want to the hawks than give it to the women or child. At last, seeing that there was no hope of their getting
any, the women went away. They built a big dardurr for themselves,
shutting themselves and the little boy up in it. Then they began singing a song which was to invoke a storm to destroy their enemies,
for so now they considered Quarrian and Gidgereegah. For some
time they chanted:

"Moogaray, Moogaray, May, May,
Eehu, Eehu, Doongarah."

First they would begin very slowly and softly, gradually getting quic-
ker and louder, until at length they almost shrieked it out. The
words they said meant, "Come hailstones; come wind; come rain;
come lightning."

While they were chanting, little Gwineeboo kept crying, and would
not be comforted. Soon came a few big drops of rain, then a big
wind, and as that lulled, more rain. Then came thunder and lightning, the air grew bitterly cold, and there came a pitiless hailstorm,
hailstones bigger than a duck's egg fell, cutting the leaves from the
trees and bruising their bark. Gidgereegah and Quarrian came running over to the dardurr and begged the women to let them in.

"No," shrieked Gwineeboo above the storm, "there was no kangaroo meat for us: there is no dardurr shelter for you. Ask shelter of the hawks whom ye fed." The men begged to be let in, said they would hunt again and get kangaroo for the women, not one but many. "No," again shrieked the women. "You would not even listen to the crying of a little child; it is better such as you should perish." And fiercer raged the storm and louder sang the women:

"Moogaray, Moogaray, May, May,
Eehu, Eehu, Doongarah."

So long and so fierce was the storm that the young men must have perished had they not been changed into birds. First they were changed into birds and afterwards into stars in the sky, where they now are, Gidgereegah and Quarrian with the kangaroo between them, still bearing the names that they bore on the earth.

MEAMEI THE SEVEN SISTERS

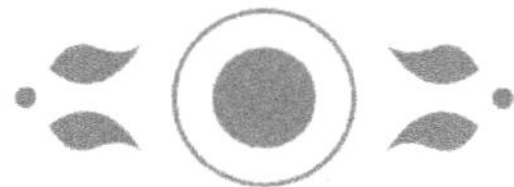

Wurrunnah had had a long day's hunting, and he came back to the camp tired and hungry. He asked his old mother for durrie, but she said there was none left. Then he asked some of the other blacks to give him some doonburr seeds that he might make durrie for himself. But no one would give him anything. He flew into a rage and he said, "I will go to a far country and live with strangers; my own people would starve me." And while he was yet hot and angry, he went. Gathering up his weapons, he strode forth to find a new people in a new country. After he had gone some distance, he saw, a long way off, an old man chopping out bees' nests. The old man turned his face towards Wurrunnah, and watched him coming, but when Wurrunnah came close to him he saw that the old man had no eyes, though he had seemed to be watching him long before he could have heard him. It frightened Wurrunnah to see a stranger having no eyes, yet turning his face towards him as if seeing him all the time. But he determined not to show his fear, but go straight on towards him, which he did. When he came up to him, the stranger told him that his name was Mooroonumildah, and that his tribe were so called because they had no eyes, but saw through their noses. Wurrunnah thought it very strange and still felt rather frightened, though Mooroonumildah seemed hospitable and kind, for he gave Wurrunnah, whom he said looked hungry, a bark wirree filled with honey, told him where his camp was, and gave him leave to go there and stay with him. Wurrunnah took the honey and turned as if to go to the camp, but when he got out of sight he thought it wiser to turn in another direction. He journeyed on for some time, until he came to a large lagoon, where he decided to camp. He took a long drink of water, and then lay down to sleep. When he woke in the morning, he looked towards the lagoon, but saw only a big plain. He thought he must be dreaming; he rubbed his eyes and looked again.

"This is a strange country," he said. "First I meet a man who has no eyes and yet can see. Then at night I see a large lagoon full of water, I wake in the morning and see none. The water was surely there, for I drank some, and yet now there is no water." As he was wondering how the water could have disappeared so quickly, he saw a big storm coming up; he hurried to get into the thick bush for shelter. When he had gone a little way into the bush, he saw a quantity of cut bark lying on the ground.

"Now I am right," he said. "I shall get some poles and with them and this bark make a dardurr in which to shelter myself from the storm I see coming."

He quickly cut the poles he wanted, stuck them up as a framework for his dardurr. Then he went to lift up the bark. As he lifted up a sheet of it he saw a strange looking object of no tribe that he had ever seen before.

This strange object cried out: "I am Bulgahnunnoo," in such a terrifying tone that Wurrunnah dropped the bark,, picked up his weapons and ran away as hard as he could, quite forgetting the storm. His one idea was to get as far as he could from Bulgahnunnoo.

On he ran until he came to a big river, which hemmed him in on three sides. The river was too big to cross, so he had to turn back, yet he did not retrace his steps but turned in another direction. As he turned to leave the river he saw a flock of emus coming to water. The first half of the flock were covered with feathers, but the last half had the form of emus, but no feathers.

Wurrunnah decided to spear one for food. For that purpose he climbed up a tree, so that they should not see him; he got his spear ready to kill one of the featherless birds. As they passed by, he picked out the one he meant to have, threw his spear and killed it, then climbed down to go and get it.

As he was running up to the dead emu, he saw that they were not emus at all but black fellows of a strange tribe. They were all standing round their dead friend making savage signs, as to what they would do by way of vengeance. Wurrunnah saw that little would avail him the excuse that he had killed the black fellow in mistake for an emu; his only hope lay in flight. Once more he took to his heels, hardly daring to look round for fear he would see an enemy behind him. On he sped, until at last he reached a camp, which he was almost into before he saw it; he had only been thinking of danger behind him, unheeding what was before him.

However, he had nothing to fear in the camp he reached so suddenly, for in it were only seven young girls. They did not look very terrifying, in fact, seemed more startled than he was. They were quite friendly towards him when they found that he was alone and hungry. They gave him food and allowed him to camp there that night. He asked them where the rest of their tribe were, and what their name was. They answered that their name was Meamei, and that their tribe were in a far country. They had only come to this country to see what it was like; they would stay for a while and then return whence they had come.

The next day Wurrunnah made a fresh start, and left the camp of the Meamei, as if he were leaving for good. But he determined to hide near and watch what they did, and if he could get a chance he would steal a wife from amongst them. He was tired of travelling alone. He saw the seven sisters all start out with their yam sticks in hand. He followed at a distance, taking care not to be seen. He saw them stop by the nests of some flying ants. With their yam sticks they dug all round these ant holes. When they had successfully unearthed the ants they sat down, throwing their yam sticks on one side, to enjoy a feast, for these ants were esteemed by them a great delicacy.

While the sisters were busy at their feast, Wurrunnah sneaked up to their yam sticks and stole two of them; then, taking the sticks with him, sneaked back to his hiding-place. When at length the Meamei had satisfied their appetites, they picked up their sticks and turned towards their camp again. But only five could find their sticks; so those five started off, leaving the other two to find theirs, supposing they must be somewhere near, and, finding them, they would soon catch them up. The two girls hunted all round the ants' nests, but could find no sticks. At last, when their backs were turned towards him, Wurrunnah crept out and stuck the lost yam sticks near together in the ground; then he slipt back into his hiding-place. When the two girls turned round, there in front of them they saw their sticks. With a cry of joyful surprise they ran to them and caught hold of them to pull them out of the ground, in which they were firmly stuck. As they were doing so, out from his hiding-place jumped Wurrunnah. He seized both girls round their waists, holding them tightly. They struggled and screamed, but to no purpose. There were none near to hear them, and the more they struggled the tighter Wurrunnah held them. Finding their screams and struggles in vain they quietened at length, and then Wurrunnah told them not to be afraid, he would take care of them. He was lonely, he said, and wanted two wives. They must come quietly with him, and he would be good to them. But they must do as he told them. If they were not quiet, he would swiftly quieten them with his moorillah. But if they would come quietly with him he would be good to them. Seeing that resistance was useless, the two young girls complied with his wish, and travelled quietly on with him. They told him that some day their tribe would come and steal them back again; to avoid which he travelled quickly on and on still further, hoping to elude all pursuit. Some weeks passed, and, outwardly, the two Meamei seemed settled down to their new life, and quite content in it, though when they were alone together they often talked of their sisters, and wondered what they had done when they realised their loss. They wondered if the five were still hunting for them, or whether they had gone back to their tribe to get assistance. That they might be in time forgotten and left with Wurrunnah for ever, they never once for a moment thought. One day when they were camped Wurrunnah said: "This fire will not burn well. Go you two and get some bark from those two pine trees over there."

"No," they said, "we must not cut pine bark. If we did, you would never more see us."

"Go! I tell you, cut pine bark. I want it. See you not the fire burns but slowly?"

"If we go, Wurrunnah, we shall never return. You will see us no more in this country. We know it."

"Go, women, stay not to talk. Did ye ever see talk make a fire burn? Then why stand ye there talking? Go; do as I bid you. Talk not so foolishly; if you ran away soon should I catch you, and, catching you, would beat you hard. Go! talk no more."

The Meamei went, taking with them their combos with which to cut the bark. They went each to a different tree, and each, with a strong hit, drove her combo into the bark. As she did so, each felt the tree that her combo had struck rising higher out of the ground and bearing her upward with it. Higher and higher grew the pine trees, and still on them, higher and higher from the earth, went the two girls. Hearing no chopping after the first hits, Wurrunnah came towards the pines to see what was keeping the girls so long. As he came near

them he saw that the pine trees were growing taller even as he looked at them, and clinging to the trunks of the trees high in the air he
saw his two wives. He called to them to come down, but they made
no answer. Time after time he called to them as higher and higher
they went, but still they made no answer. Steadily taller grew the
two pines, until at last their tops touched the sky. As they did so,
from the sky the five Meamei looked out, called to their two sisters
on the pine trees, bidding them not to be afraid but to come to
them. Quickly the two girls climbed up when they heard the voices
of their sisters. When they reached the tops of the pines the five sisters in the sky stretched forth their hands, and drew them in to live
with them there in the sky for ever.

And there, if you look, you may see the seven sisters together. You
perhaps know them as the Pleiades, but the black fellows call them
the Meamei.

MULLYANGAH THE MORNING STAR

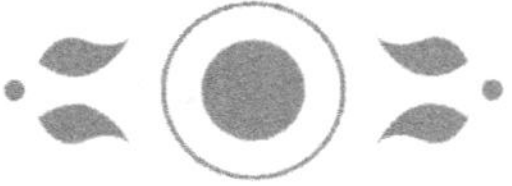

Mullyan, the eagle hawk, built himself a home high in a yaraan tree. There he lived apart from his tribe, with Moodai the opossum, his wife, and Moodai the opossum, his mother-in-law. With them too was Buttergah, a daughter of the Buggoo or flying squirrel tribe. Buttergah was a friend of Moodai, the wife of Mullyan, and a distant cousin to the Moodai tribe.

Mullyan the eagle hawk was a cannibal. That was the reason of his living apart from the other blacks. In order to satisfy his cannibal cravings, he used to sally forth with a big spear, a spear about four times as big as an ordinary spear. If he found a black fellow hunting alone, he would kill him and take his body up to the house in the tree. There the Moodai and Buttergah would cook it, and all of them would eat the flesh; for the women as well as Mullyan were cannibals. This went on for some time, until at last so many black fellows were slain that their friends determined to find out what became of them, and they tracked the last one they missed. They tracked him to where he had evidently been slain; they took up the tracks of his slayer, and followed them right to the foot of the yaraan tree, in which was built the home of Mullyan. They tried to climb the tree, but it was high and straight, and they gave up the attempt after many efforts. In their despair at their failure they thought of the Bibbees, a tribe noted for its climbing powers. They summoned two young Bibbees to their aid. One came, bringing with him his friend Murrawondah of the climbing rat tribe.

Having heard what the blacks wanted them to do, these famous climbers went to the yaraan tree and made a start at once. There was only light enough that first night for them to see to reach a fork in the tree about half-way up. There they camped, watched Mullyan away in the morning, and then climbed on. At last they reached the home of Mullyan. They watched their chance and then sneaked into his humpy.

When they were safely inside, they hastened to secrete a smouldering stick in one end of the humpy, taking care they were not seen by any of the women. Then they went quietly down again, no one the wiser of their coming or going. During the day the women heard sometimes a crackling noise, as of burning, but looking round they saw nothing, and as their own fire was safe, they took no notice, thinking it might have been caused by some grass having fallen into their fire.

After their descent from having hidden the smouldering fire stick, Bibbee and Murrawondah found the blacks and told them what they had done. Hearing that the plan was to burn out Mullyan, and fearing that the tree might fall, they all moved to some little distance, there to watch and wait for the end. Great was their joy at the thought that at last their enemy was circumvented. And proud were Bibbee and Murrawondah as the black fellows praised their prowess.

After dinner-time Mullyan came back. When he reached the entrance to his house he put down his big spear outside. Then he went in and threw himself down to rest, for long had he walked, and little had he gained. In a few minutes he heard his big spear fall down. He jumped up and stuck it in its place again. He had no sooner thrown himself down, than again he heard it fall. Once more he rose and replaced it. As he reached his resting-place again, out burst a flame of fire from the end of his humpy. He called out to the three women, who were cooking, and they rushed to help him extinguish the flames. But in spite of their efforts the fire only blazed the brighter. Mullyan's arm was burnt off. The Moodai had their feet burnt, and Buttergah was badly burnt too. Seeing they were helpless against the fire, they turned to leave the humpy to its fate, and make good their own escape. But they had left it too late. As they turned to descend the tree, the roof of the humpy fell on them. And all that remained when the fire ceased, were the charred bones of the dwellers in the yaraan tree. That was all that the blacks found of their enemies; but their legend says that Mullyan the eagle hawk lives in the sky as Mullyangah the morning star, on one side of which is a little star, which is his one arm; on the other a larger star, which is Moodai the opossum, his wife.

OUYAN THE CURLEW

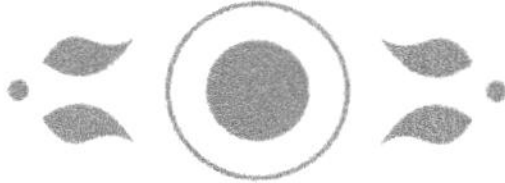

Beeargah the hawk, mother of Ouyan the curlew, said one day to her son: "Go, Ouyan, out, take your spears and kill an emu. The women and I are hungry. You are a man, go out and kill, that we may eat. You must not stay always in the camp like an old woman; you must go and hunt as other men do, lest the women laugh at you."

Ouyan took his spears and went out hunting, but though he went far, he could not get an emu, yet he dare not return to the camp and face the jeers of the women. Well could they jeer, and angry could his mother grow when she. was hungry. Sooner than return empty-handed he would cut some flesh off his own legs. And this he decided to do. He made a cut in his leg with his comebo and as he made it, cried aloud: "Yuckay! Yuckay," in pain. But he cut on, saying: "Sharper would cut the tongues of the women, and deeper would be the wounds they would make if I returned without food for them." And crying: "Yuckay, yuckay, at each stroke of his comebo, he at length cut off a piece of flesh, and started towards the camp with it.

As he neared the camp his mother cried out: "What have you brought us Ouyan?" We starve for meat, come quickly."

He came and laid the flesh at her feet, saying: "Far did I go, and little did I see, but there is enough for all to-night; to-morrow will I go forth again."

The women cooked the flesh, and ate it hungrily. Afterwards they felt quite ill, but thought it must be because they had eaten too hungrily. The next day they hurried Ouyan forth again. And again he returned bringing his own flesh back. Again the women ate hungrily of it, and again they felt quite ill.

Then, too, Beeargah noticed for the first time that the flesh Ouyan brought looked different from emu flesh. She asked him what flesh it was. He replied: "What should it be but the flesh of emu?"

But Beeargah was not satisfied, and she said to the two women who lived with her: "Go you, to-morrow, follow Ouyan, and see whence he gets this flesh."

The next day, the two women followed Ouyan when he went forth to hunt. They followed at a good distance, that he might not notice that they were following. Soon they heard him crying as if in pain: "Yuckay, yuckay, yuckay nurroo gay gay." When they came near they saw he was cutting the flesh off his own limbs. Before he discovered that they were watching him, back they went to the old woman, and told her what they had seen.

Soon Ouyan came back, bringing, as usual, the flesh with him. When he had thrown it down at his mother's feet, he went away, and lay down as if tired from the chase. His mother went up to him, and before he had time to cover his mutilated limbs, she saw that indeed the story of the women was true. Angry was she that he had so deceived her; and she called loudly for the other two women, who came running to her.

"You are right," she said. "Too lazy to hunt for emu, he cut off his own flesh, not caring that when we unwittingly ate thereof we should sicken. Let us beat him who did us this wrong."

The three women seized poor Ouyan and beat him, though he cried aloud in agony when the blows fell on his bleeding legs.

When the women had satisfied their vengeance, Beeargah said: "You Ouyan shall have no more flesh on your legs, and red shall they be for ever; red, and long and fleshless." Saying which she went, and with her the other women. Ouyan crawled away and hid himself, and never again did his mother see him. But night after night was to be heard a wailing cry of, "Bou you gwai gwai. Bou you gwai gwai," which meant, "My poor red legs. My poor red legs."

But though Ouyan the man was never seen again, a bird "with long thin legs, very red in colour under the feathers, was seen often, and heard to cry ever at night, even as Ouyan the man had cried: "Bou you gwai gwai. Bou you gwai gwai." And this bird bears always the name of Ouyan.

DINEWAN THE EMU, AND WAHN THE CROWS

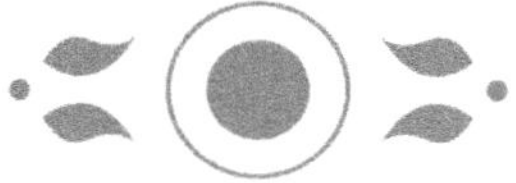

Dinewan and his two wives, the Wahn, were camping out. Seeing some clouds gathering, they made a bark humpy. It came on to rain, and they all took shelter under it. Dinewan, when his wives were not looking, gave a kick against a piece of bark at one side of the humpy, knocked it down, then told his wives to go and put it up again. While they were outside putting it up, he gave a kick, and knocked down a piece on the other side; so no sooner were they in again than out they had to go. This he did time after time, until at last they suspected him, and decided that one of them would watch. The one who was watching saw Dinewan laugh to himself and go and knock down the bark they had just put up, chuckling at the thought of his wives having to go out in the wet and cold, to put it up, while he had his supper dry and comfortably inside. The one who saw him told the other, and they decided to teach him a lesson. So in they came, each with a piece of bark filled with hot coals. They went straight up to Dinewan, who was lying down laughing. "Now," they said, "you shall feel as hot as we did cold." And they threw the coals over him. Dinewan jumped up, crying aloud with the pain, for he was badly burnt. He rolled himself over, and ran into the rain; and his wives stayed inside, and laughed aloud at him.

GOONUR, THE WOMAN-DOCTOR

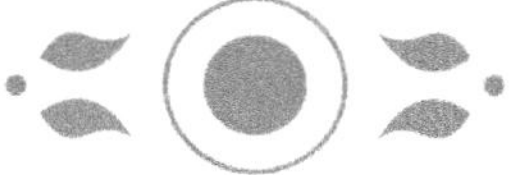

Goonur was a clever old woman-doctor, who lived with her son, Goonur, and his two wives. The wives were Guddah the red lizard, and Beereeun the small, prickly lizard. One day the two wives had done something to anger Goonur, their husband, and he gave them both a great beating. After their beating they went away by themselves. They said to each other that they could stand their present life no longer, and yet there was no escape unless they killed their husband. They decided they would do that. But how? That was the question. It must be by cunning.

At last they decided on a plan. They dug a big hole in the sand near the creek, filled it with water, and covered the hole over with boughs, leaves, and grass.

"Now we will go," they said, "and tell our husband that we have found a big bandicoot's nest."

Back they went to the camp, and told Goonur that they had seen a big nest of bandicoots near the creek; that if he sneaked up he would be able to surprise them and get the lot.

Off went Goonur in great haste. He sneaked up to within a couple of feet of the nest, then gave a spring on to the top of it. And only when he felt the bough top give in with him, and he sank down into water, did he realise that he had been tricked. Too late then to save himself, for he was drowning and could not escape. His wives had watched the success of their stratagem from a distance. When they were certain that they had effectually disposed of their hated husband, they went back to the camp. Goonur, the mother, soon missed her son, made inquiries of his wives, but gained no information from them. Two or three days passed, and yet Goonur, the son, returned not. Seriously alarmed at his long absence without having given her notice of his intention, the mother determined to follow his track. She took up his trail where she had last seen him leave the camp. This she followed until she reached the so-called bandicoot's nest. Here his tracks disappeared, and nowhere could she find a sign of his having returned from this place. She felt in the hole with her yam stick, and soon felt that there was something large there in the water. She cut a forked stick and tried to raise the body and get it out, for she felt sure it must be her son. But she could not raise it; stick after stick broke in the effort. At last she cut a midjee stick and tried with that, and then she was successful. When she brought out the body she found it was indeed her son. She dragged the body to an ant bed, and watched intently to see if the stings of the ants brought any sign of returning life. Soon her hope was realised, and after a violent twitching of the muscles her son regained consciousness. As soon as he was able to do so, he told her of the trick his wives had played on him.

Goonur, the mother, was furious. "No more shall they have you as husband. You shall live hidden in my dardurr. When we get near the camp you can get into this long, big comebee, and I will take you in. When you want to go hunting I will take you from the camp in this comebee, and when we are out of sight you can get out and hunt as of old."

And thus they managed for some time to keep his return a secret; and little the wives knew that their husband was alive and in his mother's camp. But as day after day Goonur, the mother, returned from hunting loaded with spoils, they began to think she must have help from some one; for surely, they said, no old woman could be so successful in hunting. There was a mystery they were sure, and they were determined to find it out.

"See," they said, "she goes out alone. She is old, and yet she brings home more than we two do together, and we are young. To-day she brought opossums, piggiebillahs, honey yams, quatha, and many things. We got little, yet we went far. We will watch her."

The next time old Goonur went out, carrying her big comebee, the wives watched her.

"Look," they said, "how slowly she goes. She, could not climb trees for opossums—she is too old and weak; look how she staggers."

They went cautiously after her, and saw when she was some distance from the camp that she put down her comebee. And out of it, to their amazement, stepped Goonur, their husband.

"Ah," they said, "this is her secret. She must have found him, and, as she is a great doctor, she was able to bring him to life again. We must wait until she leaves him, and then go to him, and beg to know where he has been, and pretend joy that he is back, or else surely now he is alive again he will sometime kill us."

Accordingly, when Goonur was alone the two wives ran to him, and said:

"Why, Goonur, our husband, did you leave us? Where have you been all the time that we, your wives, have mourned for you? Long has the time been without you, and we, your wives, have been sad that you came no more to our dardurr."

Goonur, the husband, affected to believe their sorrow was genuine, and that they did not know when they directed him to the bandicoot's nest that it was a trap. Which trap, but for his mother, might have been his grave.

They all went hunting together, and when they had killed enough for food they returned to the camp. As they came near to the camp, Goonur, the mother, saw them coming, and cried out:

"Would you again be tricked by your wives? Did I save you from death only that you might again be killed? I spared them, but I would I had slain them, if again they are to have a chance of killing you, my son. Many are the wiles of women, and another time I might not be able to save you. Let them live if you will it so, my son, but not with you. They tried to lure you to death; you are no longer theirs, mine only now, for did I not bring you back from the dead?

But Goonur the husband said, "In truth did you save me, my mother, and these my wives rejoice that you did. They too, as I was, were deceived by the bandicoot's nest, the work of an enemy yet to be found. See, my mother, do not the looks of love in their eyes, and words of love on their lips vouch for their truth? We will be as we have been, my mother, and live again in peace."

And thus craftily did Goonur the husband deceive his wives and make them believe he trusted them wholly, while in reality his mind was even then plotting vengeance. In a few days he had his plans ready. Having cut and pointed sharply two stakes, he stuck them firmly in the creek, then he placed two logs on the bank, in front of the sticks, which were underneath the water, and invisible. Having made his preparations, he invited his wives to come for a bathe. He said when they reached the creek:

"See those two logs on the bank, you jump in each from one and see which can dive the furthest. I will go first to see you as you come up." And in he jumped, carefully avoiding the pointed stakes. "Right," he called, "All is clear here, jump in."

Then the two wives ran down the bank each to a log and jumped from it. Well had Goonur calculated the distance, for both jumped right on to the stakes placed in the water to catch them, and which stuck firmly into them, holding them under the water.

"Well am I avenged," said Goonur. "No more will my wives lay traps to catch me." And he walked off to the camp.

His mother asked him where his wives were. "They left me," he said, "to get bees' nests."

But as day by day passed and the wives returned not, the old woman began to suspect that her son knew more than he said. She asked him no more, but quietly watched her opportunity, when her son was away hunting, and then followed the tracks of the wives. She tracked them to the creek, and as she saw no tracks of their return, she went into the creek, felt about, and there found the two bodies fast on the stakes. She managed to get them off and out of the creek, then she determined to try and restore them to life, for she was angry that her son had not told her what he had done, but had deceived her as well as his wives. She rubbed the women with some of her medicines, dressed the wounds made by the stakes, and then dragged them both on to ants' nests and watched their bodies as the ants crawled over them, biting them. She had not long to wait; soon they began to move and come to life again.

As soon as they were restored Goonur took them back to the camp and said to Goonur her son, "Now once did I use my knowledge to restore life to you, and again have I used it to restore life to your wives. You are all mine now, and I desire that you live in peace and never more deceive me, or never again shall I use my skill for you."

And they lived for a long while together, and when the Mother Doctor died there was a beautiful, dazzlingly bright falling star, followed by a sound as of a sharp clap of thunder, and all the tribes round when they saw and heard this said, "A great doctor must have died, for that is the sign." And when the wives died, they were taken up to the sky, where they are now known as Gwaibillah, the red star, so called from its bright red colour, owing, the legend says, to the red marks left by the stakes on the bodies of the two women, and which nothing could efface.

BOUGOODOOGAHDAH THE RAIN BIRD

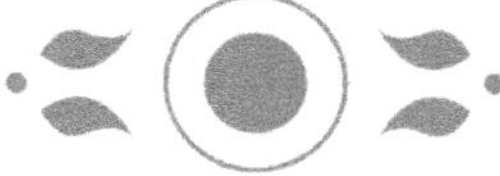

Bougoodoogahdah was an old woman who lived alone with her four hundred dingoes. From living so long with these dogs she had grown not to care for her fellow creatures except as food. She and the dogs lived on human flesh, and it was her cunning which gained such food for them all. She would sally forth from her camp with her two little dogs; she would be sure to meet some black fellows, probably twenty or thirty, going down to the creek. She would say, "I can tell you where there are lots of paddy melons." They would ask where, and she would answer, "Over there, on the point of that moorillah or ridge. If you will go there and have your nullahs ready, I will go with my two dogs and round them up towards you."

The black fellows invariably stationed themselves where she had told them, and off went Bougoodoogahdah and her two dogs. But not to round up the paddy melons. She went quickly towards her camp, calling softly, "Birree gougou," which meant "Sool 'em, sool 'em," and was the signal for the dogs to come out. Quickly they came and surrounded the black fellows, took them by surprise, flew at them, bit and worried them to death. Then they and Bougoodoogahdah dragged the bodies to their camp. There they were cooked and were food for the old woman and the dogs for some time. As soon as the supply was finished the same plan to obtain more was repeated.

The black fellows missed so many of their friends that they determined to find out what had become of them. They began to suspect the old woman who lived alone and hunted over the moorillahs with her two little dogs. They proposed that the next party that went to the creek should divide and some stay behind in hiding and watch what went on. Those watching saw the old woman advance towards their friends, talk to them for a while, and then go off with her two dogs. They saw their friends station themselves at the point of the moorillah or ridge, holding their nullahs in readiness, as if waiting for something to come. Presently they heard a low cry from the old woman of "Birree goiigou," which cry was quickly followed by dingoes coming out of the bush in every direction, in hundreds, surrounding the black fellows at the point.

The dingoes closed in, quickly hemming the black fellows in all round; then they made a simultaneous rush at them, tore them with their teeth, and killed them.

The black fellows watching, saw that when the dogs had killed their friends they were joined by the old woman, who helped them to drag off the bodies to their camp.

Having seen all this, back went the watchers to their tribe and told what they had seen. All the tribes round mustered up and decided to execute a swift vengeance. In order to do so, out they sallied well armed. A detachment went on to entrap the dogs and Bougoodoogahdah. Then just when the usual massacre of the blacks was to begin and the dogs were closing in round them for the purpose, out rushed over two hundred black fellows, and so effectual was their attack that every dog was killed, as well as Bougoodoogahdah and her two little dogs.

The old woman lay where she had been slain, but as the blacks went away they heard her cry "Bougoodoogahdah." So back they went and broke her bones, first they broke her legs and then left her. But again as they went they heard her cry "Bougoodoogahdah." Then back again they came, and again, until at last every bone in her body was broken, but still she cried "Bougoodoogahdah." So one man waited beside her to see whence came the sound, for surely, they thought, she must be dead. He saw her heart move and cry again "Bougoodoogahdah" and as it cried, out came a little bird from it. This little bird runs on the moorillahs and calls at night "Bougoodoogahdah." All day it stays in one place, and only at night comes out. It is a little greyish bird, something like a weedah. The blacks call it a rain-maker, for if any one steals its eggs it cries out incessantly "Bougoodoogahdah" until in answer to its call the rain falls. And when the country is stricken with a drought, the blacks look for one of these little birds, and finding it, chase it, until it cries aloud "Bougoodoogahdah, Bougoodoogahdah" and when they hear its cry in the daytime they know the rain will soon fall.

As the little bird flew from the heart of the woman, all the dead dingoes were changed into snakes, many different kinds, all poisonous. The two little dogs were changed into dayah minyah, a very small kind of carpet snake, non-poisonous, for these two little dogs had never bitten the blacks as the other dogs had done. At the points of the moorillahs where Bougoodoogahdah and her dingoes used to slay the blacks, are heaps of white stones, which are supposed to be the fossilised bones of the massacred men.

THE BORAH OF BYAMEE

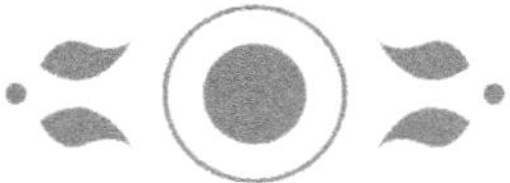

Word had been passed from tribe to tribe, telling, how that the season was good, there must be a great gathering of the tribes. And the place fixed for the gathering was Googoorewon. The old men whispered that it should be the occasion for a borah, but this the women must not know. Old Byamee, who was a great Wirreenun, said he would take his two sons, Ghindahindahmoee and Boomahoomahnowee, to the gathering of the tribes, for the time had come when they should be made young men, that they might be free to marry wives, eat emu flesh, and learn to be warriors.

As tribe after tribe arrived at Googoorewon, each took up a position at one of the various points of the ridges, surrounding the clear open space where the corrobborees were to be. The Wähn, crows, had one point; the Dummerh, pigeons, another; the Mahthi, dogs, another, and so on; Byamee and his tribe, Byahmul the black swans tribe, Oooboon, the blue tongued lizard, and many other chiefs and their tribes, each had their camp on a different point. When all had arrived there were hundreds and hundreds assembled, and many and varied were the nightly corrobborees, each tribe trying to excel the other in the fancifulness of their painted get-up and the novelty of their newest song and dance. By day there was much hunting and feasting, by night much dancing and singing; pledges of friendship exchanged, a dillibag for a boomerang, and so on; young daughters given to old warriors, old women given to young men, unborn girls promised to old men, babies in arms promised to grown men; many and diverse were the compacts entered into, and always were the Wirreenun, or doctors of the tribes consulted.

After some days the Wirreenun told the men of the tribes that they were going to hold a borah. But on no account must the innerh, or women, know. Day by day they must all go forth as if to hunt and then prepare in secret the borah ground. Out went the men each day. They cleared a very large circle quite clear, then they built an earthen dam round this circle, and cleared a pathway leading into the thick bush from the circle, and built a dam on either side of this pathway.

When all these preparations were finished, they had, as usual, a corrobboree at night. After this had been going on for some time, one of the old Wirreenun walked right away from the crowd as if he were sulky. He went to his camp, to where he was followed by another Wirreenun, and presently the two old fellows began fighting. Suddenly, when the attention of the blacks was fixed on this fight, there came a strange, whizzing, whirring noise from the scrub round. The women and children shrank together, for the sudden, uncanny, noise frightened them. And they knew that it was made by the spirits who were coming to assist at the initiation of the boys into young manhood. The noise really sounded, if you had not the dread of spirits in your mind, just as if some one had a circular piece of wood at the end of a string and were whirling it round and round.

As the noise went on, the women said, in an awestricken tone, "Gurraymy," that is "borah devil," and clutched their children tighter to them. The boys said "Gayandy," and their eyes extended with fear. "Gayandy" meant borah devil too, but the women must not even use the same word as the boys and men to express the borah spirit, for all concerning the mysteries of borah are sacred from the ears, eyes, or tongues of women.

The next day a shift was made of the camps. They were moved to inside the big ring that the black fellows had made. This move was attended with a certain amount of ceremony. In the afternoon, before the move had taken place, all the black fellows left their camps and went away into the scrub. Then just about sundown they were all to be seen walking in single file out of the scrub, along the path which they had previouly banked on each side. Every man had a fire stick in one hand and a green switch in the other. When these men reached the middle of the enclosed ring was the time for the young people and women to leave the old camps, and move into the borah ring. Inside this ring they made their camps, had their suppers and corrobboreed, as on previous evenings, up to a certain stage. Before, on this occasion, that stage arrived, Byamee, who was greatest of the Wirreenun present, had shown his power in a remarkable way. For some days the Mahthi had been behaving with a great want of respect for the wise men of the tribes. Instead of treating their sayings and doings with the silent awe the Wirreenun expect, they had kept up an incessant chatter and laughter amongst themselves, playing and shouting as if the tribes were not contemplating the solemnisation of their most sacred rites. Frequently the Wirreenun sternly bade them be silent. But admonitions were useless, gaily chattered and laughed the Mahthi. At length Byamee, mightiest and most famous of the Wirreenun, rose, strode over to the camp of Mahthi, and said fiercely to them: "I, Byamee, whom all the tribes hold in honour, have thrice bade you Mahthi cease your chatter and laughter. But you heeded me not. To my voice were added the voices of the Wirreenun of other tribes. But you heeded not. Think you the Wirreenun will make any of your tribe young men when you heed not their words? No, I tell you. From this day forth no Mahthi shall speak again as men speak. You wish to make noise, to be a noisy tribe and a disturber of men; a tribe who cannot keep quiet when strangers are in the camp; a tribe who understand not sacred things. So be it. You shall, and your descendants, for ever make a noise, but it shall not be the noise of speech, or the noise of laughter. It shall be the noise of barking and the noise of howling. And from this day if ever a Mahthi speaks, woe to those who hear him, for even as they hear shall they be turned to stone."

And as the Mahthi opened their mouths, and tried to laugh and speak derisive words, they found, even as Byamee said, so were they. They could but bark and howl; the powers of speech and laughter had they lost. And as they realised their loss, into their eyes came a look of yearning and dumb entreaty, which will be seen in the eyes of their descendants for ever. A feeling of wonder and awe fell on the various camps as they watched Byamee march back to his tribe.

When Byamee was seated again in his camp, he asked the women why they were not grinding doonburr. And the women said: "Gone are our dayoorls, and we know not where."

"You lie," said Byamee. "You have lent them to the Dummerh, who came so often to borrow, though I bade you not lend."

"No, Byamee, we lent them not."

"Go to the camp of the Dummerh, and ask for your dayoorl."

The women, with the fear of the fate of the Mahthi did they disobey, went, though well they, knew they had not lent the dayoorl. As they went they asked at each camp if the tribe there would lend them a dayoorl, but at each camp they were given the same answer, namely, that the dayoorls were gone and none knew where. The Dummerh had asked to borrow them, and in each instance been refused, yet had the stones gone.

As the women went on they heard a strange noise, as of the cry of spirits, a sound like a smothered "Oom, oom, oom, oom." The cry sounded high in the air through the tops of trees, then low on the ground through the grasses, until it seemed as if the spirits were everywhere. The women clutched tighter their fire sticks, and said: "Let us go back. The Wondah are about." And swiftly they sped towards their camp, hearing ever in the air the "Oom, oom, oom" of the spirits.

They told Byamee that all the tribes had lost their dayoorls, and that the spirits were about, and even as they spoke came the sound of "Oom, oom, oom, oom," at the back of their own camp.

The women crouched together, but Byamee flashed a fire stick whence came the sound, and as the light flashed on the place he saw no one, but stranger than all, he saw two dayoorls moving along, and yet could see no one moving them, and as the dayoorls moved swiftly away, louder and louder rose the sound of "Oom, oom, oom, oom," until the air seemed full of invisible spirits. Then Byamee knew that indeed the Wondah were about, and he too clutched his fire stick and went back into his camp.

In the morning it was seen that not only were all the dayoorls gone, but the camp of the Dummerh was empty and they too had gone. When no one would lend the Dummerh dayoorls, they had said, "Then we can grind no doonburr unless the Wondah bring us stones." And scarcely were the words said before they saw a dayoorl moving towards them. At first they thought it was their own skill which enabled them only to express a wish to have it realised. But as dayoorl after dayoorl glided into their camp, and, passing through there, moved on, and as they moved was the sound of "Oom, oom, oom, oom," to be heard everwhere they knew it was the Wondah at work. And it was borne in upon them that where the dayoorl went they must go, or they would anger the spirits who had brought them through their camp.

They gathered up their belongings and followed in the track of the dayoorls, which had cut a pathway from Googoorewon to Girrahween, down which in high floods is now a water-course. From Girrahween, on the dayoorls went to Dirangibirrah, and after them the Dummerh. Dirangibirrah is between Brewarrina and Widda Murtee, and there the dayoorls piled themselves up into a mountain, and there for the future had the blacks to go when they wanted good dayoorls. And the Dummerh were changed into pigeons, with a cry like the spirits of "Oom, oom, oom."

Another strange thing happened at this big borah. A tribe, called Ooboon, were camped at some distance from the other tribes. When any stranger went to their camp, it was noticed that the chief of the Ooboon would come out and flash a light on him, which killed him instantly. And no one knew what this light was, that carried death in its gleam. At last, Wähn the crow, said "I will take my biggest booreen and go and see what this means. You others, do not follow me too closely, for though I have planned how to save myself from the deadly gleam, I might not be able to save you."

Wahn walked into the camp of the Ooboon, and as their chief turned to flash the light on him, he put up his booreen and completely shaded himself from it, and called aloud in a deep voice 'Wah, wah, wah, wah," which so startled Ooboon that he dropt his light, and said "What is the matter? You startled me. I did not know who you were and might have hurt you, though, I had no wish to, for the Wähn are my friends,"

"I cannot stop now," said the Wähn, "I must go back to my camp, I have forgotten something I wanted to show you. I'll be back soon." And so saying, swiftly ran Wähn back to where he had left his boondee, then back he came almost before Ooboon realised that he had gone. Back he came, and stealing up behind Ooboon dealt him a blow with his boondee that avenged amply the victims of the deadly light, by stretching the chief of the Ooboon a corpse on the ground at his feet. Then crying triumphantly, "Wah, wah, wah," back to his camp went Wähn and told what he had done.

This night, when the borah corrobboree began, all the women relations of the boys to be made young men, corrobboreed all night. Towards the end of the night all the young women were ordered into bough humpies, which had been previously made all round the edge of the embankment surrounding the ring. The old women stayed on.

The men who were to have charge of the boys to be made young men, were told now to be ready to seize hold each of his special charge, to carry him off down the beaten track to the scrub. When every man had, at a signal, taken his charge on his shoulder, they all started dancing round the ring. Then the old women were told to come and say good-bye to the boys, after which they were ordered to join the young women in the humpies. About five men watched them into the humpies, then pulled the boughs down on the top of them that they might see nothing further.

When the women were safely imprisoned beneath the boughs, the men carrying the boys swiftly disappeared down the track into the scrub. When they were out of sight the five black fellows came and pulled the boughs away and released the women, who went now to their camps. But however curious these women were as to what rites attended the boys' initiation into manhood, they knew no questions would elicit any information. In some months' time they might see their boys return minus, perhaps, a front tooth, and with some extra scarifications on their bodies, but beyond that, and a knowledge of the fact that they had not been allowed to look on the face of woman since their disappearance into the scrub, they were never enlightened.

The next day the tribes made ready to travel to the place of the little borah, which would be held in about four days' time, at about ten or twelve miles distance from the scene of the big borah.

At the place of the little borah a ring of grass is made instead of one of earth. The tribes all travel together there, camp, and have a corrobboree. The young women are sent to bed early, and the old women stay until the time when the boys bade farewell to them at the big borah, at which hour the boys are brought into the little borah and allowed to say a last good-bye to the old women. Then they are taken away by the men who have charge of them together. They stay together for a short time, then probably separate, each man with his one boy going in a different direction. The man keeps strict charge of the boy for at least six months, during which time he may not even look at his own mother. At the end of about six months he may come back to his tribe, but the effect of his isolation is that he is too wild and frightened to speak even to his mother, from whom he runs away if she approaches him, until by degrees the strangeness wears off.

But at this borah of Byamee the tribes were not destined to meet the boys at the little borah. Just as they were gathering up their goods for a start, into the camp staggered Millindooloonubbah, the widow, crying, "You all left me, widow that I was, with my large family of children, to travel alone. How could the little feet of my children keep up to you? Can my back bear more than one goolay? Have I more than two arms and one back? Then how could I come swiftly with so many children? Yet none of you stayed to help me. And as you went from each water hole you drank all the water. When, tired and thirsty, I reached a water hole and my children cried for a drink, what did I find to give them? Mud, only mud. Then thirsty and worn, my children crying and their mother helpless to comfort them; on we came to the next hole. What did we see, as we strained our eyes to find water? Mud, only mud. As we reached hole after hole and found only mud, one by one my children laid down and died; died for want of a drink, which Millindooloonubbah their mother could not give them."

As she spoke, swiftly went a woman to her with a wirree of water. "Too late, too late," she said. "Why should a mother live when her children are dead?" And she lay back with a groan. But as she felt the water cool her parched lips and soften her swollen tongue, she made a final effort, rose to her feet, and waving her hands round the camps of the tribes, cried aloud: "You were in such haste to get here. You shall stay here. Googoolguyyah. Googoolguyyah. Turn into trees. Turn into trees." Then back she fell, dead. And as she fell, the tribes that were standing round the edge of the ring, preparatory to gathering their goods and going, and that her hand pointed to as it waved round, turned into trees. There they now stand. The tribes in the background were changed each according to the name they were known by, into that bird or beast of the same name. The barking Mahthi into dogs; the Byahmul into black swans; the Wähns into crows, and so on. And there at the place of the big borah, you can see the trees standing tall and gaunt, sad-looking in their sombre hues, waving with a sad wailing their branches towards the lake which covers now the place where the borah was held. And it bears the name of Googoorewon, the place of trees, and round the edge of it is still to be seen the remains of the borah ring of earth. And it is known as a great place of meeting for the birds that bear the names of the tribes of old. The Byahmuls sail proudly about; the pelicans, their water rivals in point of size and beauty; the ducks, and many others too numerous to mention. The Ooboon, or blue-tongued lizards, glide in and out through the grass. Now and then is heard the "Oom, oom, oom," of the dummerh, and occasionally a cry from the bird Millindooloonubbah of "Googoolguyyah, googoolguyyah." And in answer comes the wailing of the gloomy-looking balah trees, and then a rustling shirr through the bibbil branches, until at last every tree gives forth its voice and makes sad the margin of the lake with echoes of the past.

But the men and boys who were at the place of the little borah escaped the metamorphosis. They waited long for the arrival of the tribes who never came.

"At last," Byamee said: "Surely mighty enemies have slain our friends, and not one escapes to tell us of their fate. Even now these enemies may be upon our track; let us go into a far country."

And swiftly they went to Noondoo. Hurrying along with them, a dog of Byamee's, which would fain have lain by the roadside rather than have travelled so swiftly, but Byamee would not leave her and hurried her on. When they reached the springs of Noondoo, the dog sneaked away into a thick scrub, and there were born her litter of pups. But such pups as surely man never looked at before. The bodies of dogs, and the heads of pigs, and the fierceness and strength of devils. And gone is the life of a man who meets in a scrub of Noondoo an earmoonän, for surely will it slay him. Not even did Byamee ever dare to go near the breed of his old dog. And Byamee, the mighty Wirreenun, lives for ever. But no man must look upon his face, lest surely will he die. So alone in a thick scrub, on one of the Noondoo ridges, lives this old man, Byamee, the mightiest of Wirreenun.

DEEGEENBOYAH THE SOLDIER-BIRD

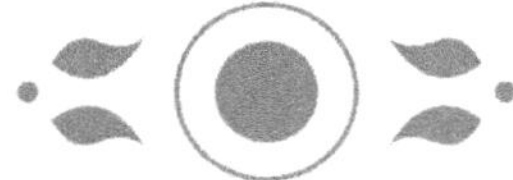

Deegeenboyah was an old man, and getting past hunting much for himself; and he found it hard to keep his two wives and his two daughters supplied with food. He camped with his family away from the other tribes, but he used to join the men of the Mullyan tribe when they were going out hunting, and so get a more certain supply of food than if he had gone by himself. One day when the Mullyan went out, he was too late to accompany them. He hid in the scrub and waited for their return, at some little distance from their camp. When they were coming back he heard them singing the Song of the Setting Emu, a song which whoever finds the first emu's nest of the season always sings before getting back to the camp. Deegeenboyah jumped up as he heard the song, and started towards the camp of the Mullyan singing the same song, as if he too had found a nest. On they all went towards the camp sing joyously:

"Nurdoo, nurbber me derreen derreenbah, ah, ah, ah, ah, ah.
Garmbay booan yunnahdeh beahwah ah, ah, ah, ah, ah.
Gubbondee, dee, ee, ee, ee.
Neäh neän gulbeejah, ah, ah, ah, ah."

Which song roughly translated means:

"I saw it first amongst the young trees,
The white mark on its forehead,
The white mark that before I had only seen as the emus moved toge-

ther in the day-time.
Never did I see one camp before, only moving, moving always.
Now that we have found the nest
We must look out the ants do not get to the eggs.
If they crawl over them the eggs are spoilt."

As the last echo of the song died away, those in the camp took up the refrain and sang it back to the hunters to let them know that they understood that they had found the first emu's nest of the season.

When the hunters reached the camp, up came Deegeenboyah too. The Mullyans turned to him, and said:

"Did you find an emu's nest too?"

"Yes," said Deegeenboyah, "I did. I think you must have found the same, though after me, as I saw not your tracks. But I am older and stiff" in my limbs, so came not back so quickly. Tell me, where is your nest?"

"In the clump of the Goolahbahs, on the edge of the plain," said the unsuspecting Mullyan.

"Ah, I thought so. That is mine. But what matter? We can share—there will be plenty for all. We must get the net and go and camp near the nest to-night, and to-morrow trap the emu."

The Mullyan got their emu trapping net, one made of thin rope about as thick as a thin clothes line, about five feet high, and between two and three hundred yards long. And off they set, accompanied by Deegeenboyah, to camp near where the emu was setting. When they had chosen a place to camp, they had their supper and a little corrobboree, illustrative of slaying emu, etc. The next morning at daylight they erected their net into a sort of triangular shaped yard, one side open. Black fellows were stationed at each end of the net, and at stated distances along it. The net was upheld by upright poles. When the net was fixed, some of the blacks made a wide circle round the emu's nest, leaving open the side towards the net. They closed in gradually until they frightened the emu off the nest. The emu seeing black fellows on every side but one, ran in that direction. The blacks followed closely, and the bird was soon yarded. Madly the frightened bird rushed against the net. Up ran a black fellow, seized the bird and wrung its neck. Then some of them went back to the nest to get the eggs, which they baked in the ashes of their fire and ate. They made a hole to cook the emu in. They plucked the emu. When they had plenty of coals, they put a thick layer at the bottom of the hole, some twigs of leaves on top of the coals, some feathers on the top of them. Then they laid the emu in, more feathers on the top of it, leaves again on top of them, and over them a thick layer of coals, and lastly they covered all with earth.

It would be several hours in cooking, so Deegeenboyah said, "I will stay and cook the emu, you young fellows take moonoons—emu spears—and try and get some more emu."

The Mullyan thought there was sense in this proposal, so they took a couple of long spears, with a jagged nick at one end, to hold the emu when they speared it; they stuck a few emu feathers on the end of each spear and went off. They soon saw a flock of emu coming past where they were waiting to water. Two of the party armed with the moonoon climbed a tree, broke some boughs and put these thickly beneath them, so as to screen them from the emu. Then as the emu came near to the men they dangled down their spears, letting the emu feathers on the ends wave to and fro. The emu, seeing the feathers, were curious as to how they got there, came over, craning their necks and sniffing right underneath the spears. The black fellows tightly grasped the moonoons and drove them with force into the two emu they had picked. One emu dropped dead at once. The other ran with the spear in it for a short distance, but the black fellow was quickly after it, and soon caught and killed it outright. Then carrying the dead birds, back they went to where Deegeenboyah was cooking the other emu. They cooked the two they had brought, and then all started for the camp in great spirits at their successful chase. They began throwing their mooroolahs as they went along, and playing with their bubberahs, or returning boomerangs. Old Deegeenboyah said, "Here, give me the emus to carry, and then you will be free to have a really good game with your mooroolahs and bubberahs, and see who is the best man."

They gave him the emus, and on they went, some throwing mooroolahs, and some showing their skill with bubberahs. Presently Deegeenboyah sat down. They thought he was just resting for a few minutes, so ran on laughing and playing, each good throw eliciting another effort, for none liked owning themselves beaten while they had a mooroolah left. As they got further away they noticed Deegeenboyah was still sitting down, so they called out to him to know what was the matter. "All right," he said, "only having a rest; shall come on in a minute." So on they went. When they were quite out of sight Deegeenboyah jumped up quickly, took up the emus and made for an opening in the ground at a little distance. This opening was the door of the underground home of the Murgah Muggui spider—the opening was a neat covering, like a sort of trap door. Down through this he went, taking the emus with him, knowing there was another exit at some distance, out of which he could come up quite near his home, for it was the way he often took after hunting.

The Mullyans went home and waited, but no sign of Deegeenboyah. Then back on their tracks they went and called aloud, but got no answer, and saw no sign. At last Mullyangah the chief of the Mullyans, said he would find him. Arming himself with his boondees and spears, he went back to where he had last seen Deegeenboyah sitting. He saw where his tracks turned off and where they disappeared, but could not account for their disappearance, as he did not notice the neat little trap-door of the Murgah Muggui. But he hunted round, determined to scour the bush until he found him. At last he saw a camp. He went up to it and saw only two little girls playing about, whom he knew were the daughters of Deegeenboyah.

"Where is your father?" he asked them.

"Out hunting," they said.

"Which way does he come home?"

"Our father comes home out of this;" and they showed him the spiders' trap-door.

"Where are your mothers?"

"Our mothers are out getting honey and yams." And off ran the little girls to a leaning tree on which they played, running up its bent trunk.

Mullyargah went and stood where the trunk was highest from the ground and said: "Now, little girls, run up to here and jump, and I will catch you. Jump one at a time."

Off jumped one of the girls towards his outstretched arms, which, as she came towards him he dropped, and, stepping aside, let her come with her full force to the ground, where she lay dead. Then he called to the horror-stricken child on the tree: "Come, jump. Your sister came too quickly. Wait till I call, then jump."

"No, I am afraid."

"Come on, I will be ready this time. Now come."

"I am afraid."

"Come on; I am strong." And he smiled quite kindly up at the child, who, hesitating no longer, jumped towards his arms, only to meet her sister's fate.

"Now," said Mullyangah, "here come the two wives. I must silence them, or when they see their children their cries will warn their husband if he is within earshot." So he sneaked behind a tree, and as the two wives passed he struck them dead with his spears. Then he went to the trapdoor that the children had shown him, and sat down to wait for the coming of Deegeenboyah. He had not long to wait. The trap-door was pushed up and out came a cooked emu, which he caught hold of and laid on one side. Deegeenboyah thought it was the girls taking it, as they had often watched for his coming and done before, so he pushed up another, which Mullyangah took, then a third, and lastly came up himself, to find Mullyangah confronting him, spear and boondee in hand. He started back, but the trap-door was shut behind him, and Mullyangah barred his escape in front.

"Ah," said Mullyangah, "you stole our food and now you shall die. I've killed your children."

Deegeenboyah looked wildly round, and, seeing the dead bodies of his girls beneath the leaning tree, he groaned aloud.

"And," went on Mullyangah, "I've killed your wives."

Deegeenboyah raised his. head and looked again wildly round, and there, on their homeward path, he saw his dead wives. Then he called aloud, "Here Mullyangah are your emus; take them and spare me. I shall steal no more, for I myself want little, but my children and my wives hungered. I but stole for them. Spare me, I pray you. I am old; I shall not live long. Spare me."

"Not so," said Mullyangah, "no man lives to steal twice from a Mullyan; "and, so saying, he speared Deegeenboyah where he stood.
Then he lifted up the emus, and, carrying them with him, went
swiftly back to his camp.

And merry was the supper that night when the Mullyans ate the
emus, and Mullyangah told the story of his search and slaughter.
And proud were the Mullyans of the prowess and cunning of their
chief.

WIRREENUN THE RAINMAKER

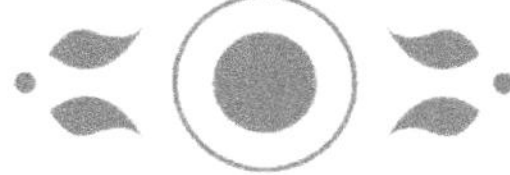

The country was stricken with a drought. The rivers were all dry except the deepest holes in them. The grass was dead, and even the trees were dying. The bark dardurr of the blacks were all fallen to the ground and lay there rotting, so long was it since they had been used, for only in wet weather did the blacks use the bark dardurr; at other times they used only whatdooral, or bough shades.

The young men of the Noongahburrah murmured among themselves, at first secretly, at last openly, saying: "Did not our fathers always say that the Wirreenun could make, as we wanted it, the rain to fall? Yet look at our country—the grass blown away, no doonburr seed to grind, the kangaroo are dying, and the emu, the duck, and the swan have flown to far countries. We shall have no food soon; then shall we die, and the Noongahburrah be no more seen on the Narrin. Then why, if he is able, does not Wirreenun make rain?"

Soon these murmurs reached the ears of the old Wirreenun. He said nothing, but the young fellows noticed that for two or three days in succession he went to the waterhole in the creek and placed in it a willgoo willgoo—a long stick, ornamented at the top with white cockatoo feathers—and beside the stick he placed two big gubberah, that is, two big, clear pebbles which at other times he always secreted about him, in the folds of his waywah, or in the band or net on his head. Especially was he careful to hide these stones from the women.

At the end of the third day Wirreenun said to the young men: "Go you, take your comeboos and cut bark sufficient to make dardurr for all the tribe."

The young men did as they were bade. When they had the bark cut and brought in Wirreenun said: "Go you now and raise with ant-bed a high place, and put thereon logs and wood for a fire, build the ant-bed about a foot from the ground. Then put you a floor of ant-bed a foot high wherever you are going to build a dardurr."

And they did what he told them. When the dardurr were finished, having high floors of ant-bed and water-tight roofs of bark, Wirreenun commanded the whole camp to come with him to the waterhole; men, women, and children; all were to come. They all followed him down to the creek, to the waterhole where he had placed the willgoo willgoo and gubberah. Wirreenun jumped into the water and bade the tribe follow him, which they did. There in the water they all splashed and played about. After a little time Wirreenun went up first behind one black fellow and then behind another, until at length he had been round them all, and taken from the back of each one's head lumps of charcoal. When he went up to each he appeared to suck the back or top of their heads, and to draw out lumps of charcoal, which, as he sucked them out, he spat into the water. When he had gone the round of all, he went out of the water. But just as he got out a young man caught him up in his arms and threw him back into the water. This happened several times, until Wirreenun was shivering. That was the signal for all to leave the creek. Wirreenun sent all the young people into a big bough shed, and bade them all go to sleep. He and two old men and two old women stayed outside. They loaded themselves with all their belongings piled up on their backs, dayoorl stones and all, as if ready for a flitting. These old people walked impatiently around the bough shed as if waiting a signal to start somewhere. Soon a big black cloud appeared on the horizon, first a single cloud, which, however, was soon followed by others rising all round. They rose quickly until they all met just overhead, forming a big black mass of clouds. As soon as this big, heavy, rainladen looking cloud was stationary overhead, the old people went into the bough shed and bade the young people wake up and come out and look at the sky. When they were all roused Wirreenun told them to lose no time, but to gather together all their possessions and hasten to gain the shelter of the bark dardurr. Scarcely were they all in the dardurrs and their spears well hidden when there sounded a terrific clap of thunder, which was quickly followed by a regular cannonade, lightning flashes shooting across the sky, followed by instantaneous claps of deafening thunder. A sudden flash of lightning, which lit a pathway from heaven to earth, was followed by such a terrific clash that the blacks thought their very camps were struck. But it was a tree a little distance off. The blacks huddled together in their dardurrs, frightened to move, the children crying with fear, and the dogs crouching towards their owners.

"We shall be killed," shrieked the women. The men said nothing but looked as frightened.

Only Wirreenun was fearless. "I will go out," he said, "and stop the storm from hurting us. The lightning shall come no nearer."

So out in front of the dardurrs strode Wirreenun, and naked he stood there facing the storm, singing aloud, as the thunder roared and the lightning flashed, the chant which was to keep it away from the camp:

"Gurreemooray, mooray,
Durreemooray, mooray, mooray," &c.

Soon came a lull in the cannonade, a slight breeze stirred the trees for a few moments, then an oppressive silence, and then the rain in real earnest began, and settled down to a steady downpour, which lasted for some days.

When the old people had been patrolling the bough shed as the clouds rose overhead, Wirreenun had gone to the waterhole and taken out the willgoo willgoo and the stones, for he saw by the cloud that their work was done.

When the rain was over and the country all green again, the blacks had a great corrobboree and sang of the skill of Wirreenun, rainmaker to the Noongahburrah.

Wirreenun sat calm and heedless of their praise, as he had been of their murmurs. But he determined to show them that his powers were great, so he summoned the rainmaker of a neighbouring tribe, and after some consultation with him, he ordered the tribes to go to the Googoorewon, which was then a dry plain, with the solemn, gaunt trees all round it, which had once been black fellows.

When they were all camped round the edges of this plain, Wirreenun and his fellow rainmaker made a great rain to fall just over the plain and fill it with water.

When the plain was changed into a lake, Wirreenun said to the young men of his tribe: "Now take your nets and fish."

"What good?" said they. "The lake is filled from the rain, not the flood water of rivers, filled but yesterday, how then shall there be fish?"

"Go," said Wirreenun. "Go as I bid you; fish. If your nets catch nothing then shall Wirreenun speak no more to the men of his tribe, he will seek only honey and yams with the women."

More to please the man who had changed their country from a de-

sert to a hunter's paradise, they did as he bade them, took their nets
and went into the lake. And the first time they drew their nets, they
were heavy with goodoo, murree, tucki, and bunmillah. And so
many did they catch that all the tribes, and their dogs had plenty.

Then the elders of the camp said now that there was plenty everywhere, they would have a borah that the boys should be made
young men. On one of the ridges away from the camp, that the women should not know, would they prepare a ground.

And so was the big borah of the Googoorewon held, the borah which
was famous as following on the triumph of Wirreenun the rainmaker.

GLOSSARY

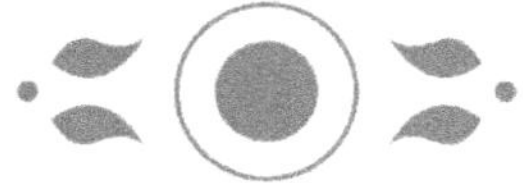

Bahloo, moon.
Beeargah, hawk.
Beeleer, black cockatoo.
Beereeun, prickly lizard.
Bibbee, woodpecker, bird.
Bibbil, shiny-leaved box-tree.
Bilber, a large kind of rat.
Billai or Billay, crimson-wing parrot.
Bindeah, a prickle or small thorn.
Bingah wingul, needle bush, a tall thorny shrub.
Birrahgnooloo, woman's name, meaning "face like a tomahawk handle."
Birrahlee, baby.
Birrahleegul, children.
Boobootella, the big bunch of feathers at the back of an emu.
Boolooral, an owl.
Boomerang, a curved weapon used in hunting and in warfare by the blacks; called Burren by the Narran blacks.
Bootoolgah, blue-grey crane.
Borah, a large gathering of blacks where the boys are initiated into the mysteries which make them young men.
Bou-gou-doo-gahdah, the rain bird. Like the bower or mocking bird.
Bouyou, legs.

Bowrah or Bohrah, kangaroo.

Bralgahs, native companion, bird.

Bubberah, boomerang that returns.

Backandee, native cat.

Buggoo, flying squirrel.

Bulgahnunnoo, bark-backed.

Bumble, a fruit-bearing tree, sometimes called wild orange and sometimes wild pomegranate tree. Capparis.

Bunbundoolooey, brown flock pigeon.

Bunnyyarl, flies.

Burreenjin, magpie, lark, or peewee.

Budtha, rosewood-tree, also girl's name.

Byamee, man's name, meaning "big man,'"

Comebee, bag made of kangaroo shins.

Comeboo, stone tomahawk.

Cookooburrah, laughing jackass.

Coorigil, name of place, meaning sign of bees.

Corrobboree, black fellows' dance.

Cunnembeillee, woman's name, meaning pig-weed root.

Curree guin guin, butcher-bird.

Daen, black fellows.

Dardurr, bark, humpy or shed.

Dayah minyah, carpet snake.

Dayoorl, large flat stone for grinding grass-seed upon.

Deegeenboyah, soldier-bird.

Deereeree, willy wagtail.

Dheal, the sacred tree of the Noongahburrahs, only used for putting on the graves of the dead.

Dinewan, emu.

Dingo, native dog.

Doonburr, a grass seed.

Doongara, lightning.

Dummerh, pigeons.

Dungle, water hole.

Dunnia, wattle.

Durrie, bread made from grass seed.

Eär moonän, long sharp teeth.

Euloo marah, large tree grubs. Edible.

Euloo wirree, rainbow.

Galah or Gilah, a French grey and rose-coloured cockatoo.

Gayandy, borah devil.

Gidgereegah, a species of small parrot.

Girrahween, place of flowers.

Gooeea, warriors.

Googarh, iguana.

Googoolguyyah, turn into trees.

Googoorewon, place of trees,

Goolahbah, grey-leaved box-tree.

Goolahgool, water-holding tree.

Goolahwilleel, top-knot pigeon.

Gooloo, magpie.

Goomade, red stump,

Goomai, water rat.

Goomblegubbon, bustard or plain turkey.

Goomillah, young girl's dress, consisting of waist strings made of opossum's sinews with strands of woven opossum's hair hanging about a foot square in front.

Goonur, kangaroo rat.

Goug gour gahgah, laughing jackass. Literal meaning, "Take a stick."

Grooee, handsome foliaged tree bearing a plum-like fruit, tart and bitter, but much liked by the blacks.

Gubberah, magical stones of Wirreenun. Clear crystallised quatty.

Guddah, red lizard.

Guiebet, a thorny creeper bearing masses of a lovely myrtle-like flower and an edible fruit somewhat resembling passion fruit.

Guinary, light eagle hawk.

Guineeboo, robin redbreast.

Gurraymy, borah devil.

Gwai, red.

Gwaibillah, star. Mars.

Kurreah, an alligator.

Mahthi, dog.

Maimah, stones.

Maira, paddy melon.

May or Mayr, wind.

Mayrah, spring wind.

Meamei, girls.

Midjee, a species of acacia.

Millair, species of kangaroo rat.

Moodai, opossum.

Moogaray, hailstones.

Mooninguggahgul, mosquito-calling bird.

Moonoon, emu spear.

Mooregoo, mopoke.

Mooroonumildah, having no eyes.

Morilla or Moorillah, pebbly ridges.

Mubboo, beef wood-tree.

Mullyan, eagle hawk.

Mullyangah, the morning star.

Murgah muggui, big grey spider.

Murrawondah, climbing rat.

Narahdarn, bat.

Noongahburrah, tribe of blacks on the Narran.

Nullah nullah, a club or heavy-headed weapon.

Nurroo gay gay, dreadful pain.

Nyunnoo or Nunnoo, a grass, humpy.

Ooboon, blue-tongued lizard.

Oolah, red prickly lizard.

Oongnairwah, black diver.

Ouyan, curlew.

Piggiebillah, ant-eater. One of the Echidna, a marsupial.

Quarrian, a kind of parrot.

Quatha, quandong; a red fruit like a round red plum.

U e hu, rain, only so called in song.

Wahgoo, to hide. A game like hide-and-seek.

Wahroogah, children.

Wahn, crow.

Wayambeh, turtle.

Waywah, worn by men, consisting of a waistband made of opossum's sinews with bunches of strips of paddy melon skins hanging from it.

Weedah, bower or mocking-bird.

Weeoombeen, a small bird. Some thing like a redbreast, only with longer tail and not so red a breast.

Widya nurrah, a wooden battle-axe shaped weapon.

Willgoo willgoo, painted stick with feathers on top.

Wirree, small piece of bark, canoe-shaped.

Wirreenun, priest or doctor.

Womba, mad.

Wondah, spirit or ghost.

Wurranunnah, wild bees.

Wurrawilberoo, whirlwind with a devil in it; also clouds of Magellan.

Wurranunnah, bee.

Wurrunnah, man's name, meaning standing.

Yaraan, white gum-tree.

Yhi, the sun.

Yuckay, oh dear!